Equal Shares

Oodi Weavers and the Cooperative Experience

Dennis Lewycky & Keitseope Nthomang

Between the Lines
Toronto, Canada

Equal Shares: Oodi Weavers and the Cooperative Experience
© 1999 Dennis Lewycky & Keitseope Nthomang

Between the Lines gratefully acknowledges financial assistance for our publishing activities from the Ontario Arts Council, The Canada Council for the Arts, and the Government of Canada through the Book Publishing Industry Development Program.

Every reasonable effort has been made to find copyright holders. The publisher would be pleased to have any errors or omissions brought to its attention.

Canadian Cataloguing in Publication Data

Lewycky, Dennis
    Equal shares

Includes bibliographical references.
ISBN 1-896357-21-0

·1. Lentswe la Oodi Weavers (Association). 2. Textile cooperatives — Botswana — Oodi. 3. Rural development — Botswana — Oodi. I. Nthomang, Keitseope. II. Title.

HD8039.T42B67 1999   331.7'677'0096883   C99-930136-5

Colour photos 1997 by Dennis Lewycky
Black and white photos 1977 by Dennis Lewycky
Black and white photos 1974 by Sandy Grant
Cover Design: Margie Adam, ArtWork, Toronto
Interior Design: Steve Izma

Printed in Canada by Transcontinental Printing

1 2 3 4 5 6 7 8 9 10   05 04 03 02 01 00 99

Between the Lines
720 Bathurst Street, #404, Toronto, Ontario, M5S 2R4, Canada
(416) 535-9914 www.btl.on.ca   btlbooks@web.net

Contents

Acknowledgements

I must thank the weavers for sharing their knowledge and allowing me to work with them to write this book. Their hospitality and acceptance of me are truly appreciated. Others I must thank include Sandy and Elinah Grant, who opened up their home and thoughts to me and were extremely provocative in developing my thinking about how the Cooperative is functioning within the Botswana environment. Keitseope Nthomang, my co-author, played an important role in setting up the research in Botswana, participating in key discussions with the weavers, guiding my thinking, and writing material for the book. Peder Gowenius, Ulla Gowenius, and Joan Hoff also provided me with important insights and judgements on the weavers' experience.

In Canada I received a great deal of useful support and critical input from a number of people with an interest and affection for the weavers. Thank you to all! Particularly helpful were Helmut and Marlyn Kuhn, who were instrumental in getting the project started in 1973 with the Goweniuses. Lucie Brunet provided substantial editorial and analytical guidance. And a special thanks goes to Gisele Morin-Labatut at IDRC who found funding to support the research for this book. She continues to support people around the world whose efforts do not fit neatly into the programme priorities of development agencies, but who have quietly toiled at social change with principle and passion.

Lentswe la Oodi Producers Cooperative
P.O. Box 954
Oodi, Kgatleng District, BOTSWANA

Dennis Lewycky
2235 Harding Road,
Ottawa, CANADA K1G 3B3
commgroup@magi.com

September 1998

Chronology of Significant Events

1972   Peder and Ulla Gowenius arrive in Botswana
1973   Weavers project proposal approved by government
        Construction on the factory buildings starts
        The first weavers are hired and start their training
1974   Oodi Weavers is officially opened
1977   Evaluation of the weavers — *Tapestry, Report from Oodi Weavers*
1978   The Goweniuses leave Oodi
1979   Ulla Gowenius returns for three months of upgrading
1980   Oodi Weavers is registered as a producers cooperative
1982   CORDE conducts an assessment of the management
1983   Peder Gowenius returns for a brief visit
1985   Two Swedish weavers start a diversification effort
1986   Exhibits of tapestries tour Sweden, Denmark, and Canada
1987   Oodi tapestries tour Saskatchewan
1992   A group of village leaders offers to help the weavers
1993   The Consumers Cooperative closes
        Revenues cannot pay for salaries for six month
1994   Joan Hoff, Peace Corps volunteer, arrives
        Setsuko Takazawa, Japanese volunteer, arrives

1996   Sandy Grant offers to buy Oodi Weavers
       Joan Hoff leaves
1997   Research for this book conducted
       Japanese volunteer replaced
       Meeting with village leaders takes place

Introduction

At the centre of this book are 32 people who own and operate the Lentswe la Oodi Producers Cooperative (Oodi Weavers). With minimal formal education, virtually no job experience, no background in workers cooperatives, still working their agricultural lands — in many cases as single mothers — they have maintained their "factory" for 25 years in the village of Oodi, Botswana. They provide the physical energy, production skills, and constant optimism that have driven the Cooperative forward.

The workers — 30 women and two men — who labour at the factory have demonstrated perseverance and patience. Day after day they sit at their looms to produce beautiful woven wool products. They have weathered near collapses and have gone through phases of growth and decline. At the same time they have managed to bring up their children, meet family and village obligations, and generally improve their quality of life. The workers have been the stalwart constants within a process of prodigious economic and social change in their community and nation.

This book tells a story of how the weavers have beaten the odds and how they have "done things wrong" and yet succeeded where others failed. As a group of villagers they did not seem to have a lot to offer the project, and there was limited optimism in higher levels of government that they could succeed. They have followed cooperative and business requirements to some degree but most of the time they have created their own operational method, an ad hoc style that has managed to keep the factory going.

Written in different voices, this story offers the defining moments and abstract relations that make up the life of Oodi Weavers. Often this life is confused and complex as the workers have tried to manage the factory in their own eclectic and spontaneous manner. The story of Oodi Weavers also has its tedious moments, just as there are endless hours of hand-stressing labour within each beautiful tapestry produced.

What the Oodi experience reveals, as a main link in a mix of factors, is that commitment to a cause — with its related motivation and tenacity — is a key requirement for a sustained community economic development (CED) enterprise. Because a core group of about 12 to 15 women believe the factory is theirs and that ownership is a real opportunity and obligation, they have the commitment and motivation to persist. They know the factory depends on them to survive. They have demonstrated the determination and dedication needed to maintain production through the good and bad times.

The narrative in the following pages will weave a tapestry-like story of lessons and challenges, a story that depicts the weavers' evolving collective experience in all its local colour.

The Beginnings of Oodi Weavers

The story of the weavers' efforts and this book starts in 1972, when a Swedish family, Peder and Ulla Gowenius and their two sons, Pule and Siza, came to Botswana. They suggested the idea of a weaving project to government officials and local non-governmental organization (NGO) representatives. Through a convoluted and at times frustrating process, they arranged initial support for the project and were instrumental in starting the "factory," as it is called by the workers. Without a doubt, they provided the project with its unique organizational and developmental character.

In 1977, I was hired by CUSO (Canadian University Service Overseas), an initial donor, to evaluate the project with the workers. Over a six-month period, through a participatory evaluation method, we analysed the development of the project with all its strengths and weaknesses. The results were documented in *Tapestry, Report from Oodi Weavers*. This detailed account was widely read throughout Africa because of the wealth of knowledge reflected in it, written in the weavers' and villagers' own words. Twenty years later, I initiated a return to the village of Oodi to write about the people and the project again, this time with a global and more mature understanding of development issues. Financial help for this return visit came from the International Development Research Centre (IDRC).

I believe the weavers have achieved a great deal in this development project, although it is a complicated and qualified achievement. The fact that the Cooperative is still functioning after so many years is significant when we think of the hundreds of similar initiatives — rural projects, producer cooperatives, village industries, small community businesses — that have not continued to operate.

I am reluctant to say these other projects have failed. Many projects may not continue as planned but still achieve a great deal in terms of individual or spin-off benefits. However, the history of international development is littered with collapsed production projects, so it is encouraging to read about how some ventures do continue and why they are able to do so. Regardless of formal outcomes, these productive ventures significantly contribute to the overall development and quality of life in their communities, and are, therefore, instructive for others working in the field of rural development or village revitalization.

This book will describe and examine the Lentswe la Oodi Producers Cooperative so that others, across Africa and elsewhere, who are interested in community-based strategies for social change, can learn from their experience. While the weavers and their story are situated in Botswana, I believe they can encourage and challenge us to think about issues that have a far more universal appeal and application. Their experience does not provide us with a crystal ball but it does supply a relevant prism through which we can view our own ideas and actions.

Practical and Philosophical Issues

The weavers have operated the factory for 25 years, which provides a serious time frame within which they have tried and tested various aspects of running a production cooperative. We have the luxury of viewing practical and philosophical issues of development as they exist rather than only speculating about them as we normally must do when starting such projects. Also, the participants are applying critically important ownership and management techniques, which are being implemented all over the world but which are still evolving and, therefore, in need of ongoing reflection and debate. And although the weavers' social relations are unique to their situation, their example helps us to reflect on our own relations. This is particularly important when people of one culture intervene in another community's or country's social and economic development.

There is a great deal more that could be learned from the workers on why they have stayed with the Cooperative for so many years, why some have left, what impact the factory has had on the individuals involved, what alternatives and options were available to the weavers, and on and on. As most of the workers are women, there is also much that could be learned about how women function within and benefit from such community-based enterprises in the African context. However, I did not conduct this kind of research and the weavers did not engage in a formal evaluation of their work.

Community Economic Development

The Weavers Cooperative, this village industry, is what we in Canada call a community economic development (CED) venture, and in other parts of the world it is referred to as a social economy project or community enterprise. CED is a strategy for improving the quality of life for people who have been socially and economically exploited or denied access to the various developments that some others in their countries have enjoyed. This should not be a restrictive label or another glib acronym to isolate what the weavers are doing. Situating the weavers in a broader phenomenon of planned change that is global and yet rooted in the daily lives of people living in poverty is a device for describing and understanding the weavers' experience. Examining the weavers through the CED prism allows us to identify key dynamics and relations that are important to the weavers' experience. This information can be used by other people who are interested in their own development.

The book is written mainly from the point of view of the workers in the Cooperative and people who have worked with them since the beginning of the project. I have followed the life of the Cooperative and, from my experience of community economic development in different countries, have written to complement their experience. Keitseope Nthomang, a Motswana academic who is actively involved in village revitalization efforts in Botswana, has written a chapter on the Botswana context, and he has advised me throughout the writing process. This mix of perspectives is intended to help others who are interested in practical involvement in similar ventures, in funding them, or in creating the policy support that will facilitate their operations.

Therefore, the substance of the book focuses on what the weavers can tell or teach us about setting up and operating a CED venture, whether in Africa or in any underdeveloped part of the world. I try to explain what the project has achieved, what problems have arisen, and what has been done to support the Cooperative. Ultimately I hope that the weavers' experience challenges us all in what we think and do as part of our roles in supporting rural or village development initiatives.

Though the weavers are organized as a producer cooperative (also called worker or industrial cooperative), the project has social and developmental objectives and that is why we are using a CED frame of analysis rather than a production cooperative framework. However, much of what we include in this book will parallel what advocates of producer cooperatives find relevant.

Lessons in Structure and Culture

To simplify what the weavers can teach us, I have separated their experience into two basic dimensions that I think characterize all CED ventures and that can reveal useful lessons for replication. The first dimension is the structural one: functional or concrete major requirements. The second is cultural: how process relations are understood and organized. While these dimensions are obviously related and interlinked, they denote different aspects of a community-based venture and rely on different approaches to their applications.

The structural dimension of a CED enterprise includes development capital, knowledgeable workers, and profitable markets, which are technical in nature and often tied to what other partners in development can provide. No CED venture can operate without these supports but each community or group of people will use them according to their circumstances. To some degree these requirements are similar to what small businesses or private entrepreneurs have to deal with, and banks and technical assistance agencies are familiar with providing their support based on this structural information.

The cultural dimension includes the cooperative values, leadership, and management features, which are variable and unique to a people and a place. These features define the ongoing and numerous relationships involved in CED ventures. While I think these relations are equally important to the structural dimension and to some degree are universally found in CED ventures, they depend more on how the people involved in a venture apply them or adapt them. Personal factors and social complexities of the group also come into play. For any effort that seeks social change, it is at this level that such amorphous factors as intuition, chance, and judgement make a difference.

Chapter by Chapter

Chapter 1 describes the Cooperative, primarily as it is today but also as it was when it began and through some of its history in between. This description also features insightful comments by the weavers so that they start telling their story by sharing their views and perspectives.

The second chapter is an account of the project history, with details of how it was designed and promoted to key supporters, and how the Botswana government became involved.

Chapter 3 rounds out the description of the project with a look at the Botswana context, village background, and national character that has been the historical and demographic framework for the Oodi Weavers' tapestry.

The second section of the book shifts to a more analytical position, first from the point of view of the weavers and the managers of the project in 1977. The content of chapter 4 is largely drawn from the evaluation they completed in that year and, therefore, it reflects what they were concerned with as they started the project.

Chapter 5 explores how the Cooperative has benefited the weavers. It includes interviews with three women (two weavers and a village leader) in 1997. These women were also interviewed in 1977.

Chapter 6, written from a CED point of view, includes my analysis of what we can universally extract from the weavers' experience. In this chapter I elaborate on a number of formative issues that CED practitioners face in their work and look at how the weavers have dealt with these issues.

Part *1*

The Practice

Chapter 1

Lentswe la Oodi Producers Cooperative

*E*arly each morning, five days a week, a group of village women converge at the lowest end of the village of Oodi. The Lentswe la Oodi Producers Cooperative is located there, 30 kilometres northeast of Gaborone, Botswana's capital city. The 30 women usually sing a couple of hymns or say a short prayer before they disburse to their looms or spinning wheels to become weavers.

The main building in the Cooperative's compound is a rectangular cement-block structure with a one-sided peaked roof. The numerous openings below the roof peak allow a constant breeze to cool the interior in summer, though the workspace can be quite cold in winter. Painted a buoyant white with Mediterranean blue trim, the building complements the sales shop nearby, which was constructed in a more traditional Batswana style, with a grass-thatched roof and rounded walls. Hidden to the back of the compound, behind an outcrop of huge grey granite, is another distinctive thatched building. This was built as a

Terminology Note: The country is Botswana, the people are Batswana, an individual is a Motswana, and the language spoken is Setswana.

All financial information in the book is denoted in pula (P), the national currency of Botswana. One pula traded at Can$0.35 or US$0.28 in April 1997.

home for the first managers of the Cooperative and their family; then for a few years it was a showroom for the Cooperative. This unique building now stands vacant and is slowly decaying. A small rondavel, a traditional Batswana house, is also nestled between the rock bulge and the open veldt that spreads out quietly behind the Cooperative.

Wool is dyed on an external stove near the main building. Huge bundles of wool that hang to dry in the intense African sun create splashes of vibrant colour — blue, red, orange, brown — in lively contrast to the seasonal green or yellow of the village landscape.

The atmosphere in the factory is always gently animated. Constant laughter and conversation play to the rhythmic slap of the floor looms, as the workers weave or move casually around the workplace. When customers arrive, the noise level drops as a couple of the weavers engage the visitors for a few minutes. Most of the workers sit at their tapestry or floor looms or at the finishing table in the middle of the building, though in the winter some of them will keep warm by moving the stand-alone looms outside into the sun.

At noon, the piercing twang of a steel triangle announces the end of the morning's work and the weavers stream out of the factory. Most walk home for their midday meal while those from the nearby villages of Modipane and Matebele eat at the factory. The compound takes on a drowsy atmosphere in the heat. The return to work is not as uniform, but by shortly after two o'clock all the workers are back at their looms, spinning wheels, or tables, and the murmur of socializing can once again be heard like a horizon above the quiet of the village. At five in the afternoon, another twang announces the end of their work day.

For 25 years, Oodi Weavers have been generating beautiful woven crafts and a great deal of public interest in Botswana. Their woolen products can be found in homes, offices, and embassies around the world. Their tapestries have given Batswana a creative reflection of themselves for others to admire. For those involved in international development practice and issues, the weavers are seen as either a development icon, because of their achievements and longevity, or an iconoclastic development, since the Cooperative has been able to provide an income for the members in a way that no other venture in Botswana has been able to do.

This chapter describes some key features of the weavers' project, how the workers relate to each other, and how the enterprise has changed over the years. It provides the scope and detail needed to appreciate how and why the weavers have functioned. While the chapter is largely descriptive, it is also full of individual reflections and facts.

Who Are the Weavers?

Initially, in 1973, there were 52 people taking part in the production process of the factory. Ninety per cent of them were women and they ranged in age from 20 to 50, though most were in their 40s. Because the project was intended to assist three neighbouring villages, workers were proportionally selected from Oodi (74 per cent), Matebele (13 per cent), and Modipane (13 per cent). The number of workers has fluctuated over the years, and in 1997 there were 32 members (only two were men) though there was roughly the same village distribution as there was at the beginning. The youngest and most recent villager to join the factory is 19 years old.

Though individuals may have multiple duties within the factory, there are usually three or four spinners, eight or nine spread weavers, 16 tapestry weavers, four workers finishing off the products, four dying or preparing the bobbins, and two in management positions. In addition to the weavers, in 1997 there were two cleaners, two night watchmen, and a driver, working for the weavers but not members of the Cooperative.

About 20 of the workers have been with the firm since it was set up. Others have joined at different times, either when a weaver left and was replaced by a relative (which was encouraged by the weavers) or as production opportunities warranted. For example, between 1995 and 1996, when a Peace Corps volunteer was able to bolster sales of the tapestries, seven weavers (new and returning) started work.

All the weavers maintain agricultural lands near their villages and about half also have a cattle post where they keep livestock. About two-thirds of the women are married and all the weavers have children to care for. Only a few have had any formal education beyond primary school, with some having no schooling at all. Most have never had previous paid employment other than working as domestic servants or nannies in Gaborone or South Africa.

As *Tapestry, Report from Oodi Weavers* recorded in 1977,

> Before the factory came into existence, most of [the workers] were employed at menial labour, such as housekeeping, or in mining, and without the factory most said they would return to these positions outside their village. Therefore, the factory work has given this relatively disadvantaged group increased opportunity in the village environment they stated clearly they preferred. . . . A group within the workers is also the

most economically depressed group within Botswana. Over 40 per cent of the women in the factory are the heads of households and these women throughout the nation are less economically secure, have the lowest employment potential and generally are the most dependent on external assistance. For these women and their children (an average of three), the factory has released them from possible suffering and insecurity (note that half of those in the factory who said they built new houses since 1975 were women household heads). (Lewycky 1977 and 1981, 222)

Three of the workers have died since the late 1980s; four others retired because the work was too strenuous for their age; and a couple said they had other family obligations that prevented them from continuing to work.

Some of the workers reportedly left the Cooperative because they could earn more money elsewhere. In the years between 1979 and 1984, for example, 14 workers left, and during a "collapse" of the Cooperative between 1988 and 1994 another 15 workers terminated their work. Since many of these former weavers are no longer living in Oodi, it is difficult to determine accurately why they left the Cooperative. In interviews, five former workers still living in Oodi said they left because of low wages paid by the Cooperative.

All of the men who had started working at the factory left during these two periods, though one returned and is now a member of the Cooperative. Although low wages contributed to their departures, a couple of the weavers noted that some of the men would quarrel with the managers as they did not like to work "under women." As former weaver and bookkeeper Mmapala Moeng said, "As you know, in the management committee it is women, and if we say that the men should come on time or improve the quality of their work they will just say, 'Ah, she is just a woman; what is she trying to say?' They may even abscond from duties without a reason. . . . If he is confronted about not coming to work for many days, he would just say, 'Ah you know nothing; I was just attending to my family matters.'"

Beautiful Woven Products

The workers at the factory produce woven woolen articles such as tapestries, bedspreads, wall hangings, tablecloths, table place mats, and women's jackets. Each item is handmade by the weavers and is, therefore, unique in design, size, and colour.

Tapestries

The tapestries that depict individual stories or scenes about some aspect of a weaver's experience or Botswana life are probably the best known product and the most popular with customers. In a 1987 catalogue promoting the weavers, Ann Newdigate Mills wrote,

> The urgency and vision of the Oodi tapestries combined with their technical and aesthetic confidence can be envied by graduates of Canadian art institutions. One of the strengths of the Oodi tapestries is their ability to use the most simple process to such great advantage. Yet the content and composition are by no means simple.

General village scenes and the daily concerns of growing food, raising children, or maintaining social customs are common themes. Other tapestries depict scenes that comment on the problems and dynamics of change experienced by a developing nation. In the 1970s, for example, a frequent theme was male migration to South African mines, which left the women to struggle alone at their homes. With the liberation struggles in neighbouring Zimbabwe and South Africa, some weavers commented on the sources of conflict in these countries and expressed a need for political action. Some of the titles of the early tapestries were the Soweto riots, free Nelson Mandela, the South African mines, independence for Mozambique, and women's oppression.

While the village scenes seemed popular and in demand, there was some concern about the lack of variety in their designs. As weaver Tidimalo Tlhagwane commented, "We only did one thing, village life, village life."

Because of tourist demand, many of the current tapestries contain wildlife and, particularly, exotic animal scenes with lions, zebras, and elephants. These have been difficult for the weavers to create, since most of them have never seen any of the wildlife that they are weaving into their designs. If a client has a particular theme in mind (for example, local churches have ordered tapestries for their congregations), the weavers will respond to custom orders as well.

No tradition of this kind of weaving exists in Botswana, though in the north of the country there are people skilled at weaving grass mats and other utility objects. However, a tradition of home decoration and painting has provided design and colour references for the weavers (Grant and Grant 1995).

Other Items

Carpets tend to be more expensive to manufacture because of the quantity of wool used. They sold for P35 per metre in 1980 but were discontinued by the mid-1980s because, according to the current manager, there was not a strong demand for them.

In 1976 the weavers started producing other smaller woven items such as pillows, handbags, table mats, and wall hangings. The production of these and the runners was initiated to make use of unoccupied looms and to utilize workers who had not achieved proficiency standards in tapestries or bedspreads. Also, the management thought that diversity would offer the customer more of a selection and could cater to a lower-income clientele. Another effort to diversify the weavers' products was initiated between 1985 and 1988 with the support of the Swedish International Development Agency (SIDA). A line of clothing (including belts, bags, jackets, ponchos, and hats) was created and sold until the early 1990s. Only the jackets are still currently being made and sell for about P350 each.

In 1994 the weavers tried to expand production into a line of school uniforms. A few local young women were trained to sew and a small grant was obtained from the government to buy sewing machines. The effort failed after a few months because no one was able to manage the group or had the technical knowledge to deal with production problems that arose.

The factory showroom displays other items that are sold by the weavers but made by other Batswana craftspeople. For example, woven grass mats and bowls made by people from the Kalahari Desert are sold, as are small dolls dressed in traditional African costumes, which are made by a woman who lives in Oodi. In the early years the weavers also marketed small wood furniture that was made on site by a couple of men who had received a loan to start a small carpentry business on the weavers' site.

Quality Raw Materials

All of the raw materials used in the various articles are imported into Botswana. Originally, the weavers used Marino wool from England and linen warp from Ireland. Today they obtain the less expensive and equally malleable Corriedale wool and all other requirements, such as dye and related chemicals, from South Africa.

Once the wool is received in bulk, it is spun and dyed according to the needs of the particular weaves or to individual requests of the weavers. It is also treated against deterioration by insect infestation. Requests to purchase the high-quality spun and dyed wool from the factory have been turned down so far, but this product may join others in the showroom in the future.

The tapestries are woven on 16 vertical frames. The bedspreads, runners, and tablecloths are woven on ten wooden floor looms. The early weaves of these latter products had traditional Batswana designs in a variety of colours. Others have a plain design or representations of rondavels with vibrant and varied colours that were added later. Because of the high quality of the weaving and the attractive patterns, many of the spreads are used for wall hangings. They sell at prices from P290 to P500 each (according to the size, design complexity, and quality). The runners cost between P10 and P135. The tapestries sell for P650 a square metre and range in size from one to four square metres.

Selling the Goods

Over 80 per cent of the woven items are sold from the sales building at the factory location in Oodi. Visitors can search through a varied stock of products and are also able to see the weavers at work. The balance of their stock is sold in Gaborone through two commercial outlets (the Gaborone Sun Hotel and Botswanacraft, the government's craft marketing agency) or directly overseas according to orders. (A special tapestry of almost 12 square metres was woven for the U.S. Embassy in Gaborone.) With the help of the Department of Cooperative Development and the Ministry of Commerce and Industry, the weavers participate in the agricultural fairs and trade shows held in Gaborone annually, where their sales have been modest. Very little effort is made to sell products through other distributors or to market the crafts elsewhere in Botswana.

In general, there has not been a concerted effort to develop external markets, mainly because existing sales have kept up with production. There are also tariff and exporting costs on articles, which the weavers feel make these markets less commercially viable. In 1986, major efforts were made to exhibit and sell Oodi weaves in Sweden, Denmark, and Canada, and these efforts were very profitable, but nothing similar has been explored since then. Those exhibits were organized by supporters of the weavers in the various countries, with very little effort on the part of the weavers.

Currently, there are an average of 100 visitors to the factory every month, most of whom are tourists or foreigners working in Botswana.

While monthly sales can vary to a large degree, sales for the first three months of 1997 were P8,800, P16,500, and P15,400, which can give some indication of the level of output. Because most of the woven products are considered expensive for a local market, there is very little merchandise sold to the villagers or to Batswana living in Gaborone.

"We just wait for customers to come to the factory," reported weaver Tsietsi Mogapi. "We don't plan for the future, because we don't have an idea of what to do. We work in the factory, in groups, but we all have our own minds; our opinions are not the same and we don't agree, so we end up arguing. This stops our progress."

Worker Training

The technical and artistic skills training within the factory was initially done by Ulla Gowenius (known as Mma Masiza in Setswana). Being a trained and experienced weaver, she provided the intensive training for each type of production skill as the workers entered the factory. This training was conducted in six groups of 12 persons in late 1973 and early 1974.

An important part of the weavers' training was to cultivate a social awareness and an understanding of development issues. From the day the weavers entered the factory they were confronted by the Goweniuses talking about worker control, exploitation, oppression, cooperative spirit, and social commitment. When learning about industrialization, for example, they heard of the exploitation that accompanied it in Europe. When discussing story ideas to weave into tapestries, they considered the economic basis for racism, why men were attracted to the South African mines, and how villagers could contribute to national development goals.

Skills Training

Training for each type of skill — spinning, tapestry, or loom weaving — began with a lecture on the history of textiles and the relationship between the sources of raw materials and the processes leading to a final woven article. This included a description of the evolution of clothing from skins to modern synthetics, and the intervention of industrialization in the production of textiles and, therefore, the competition between mass-produced and individually made materials. "We tried to show that people would pay for something that is unique. That there are people who want something different. Therefore, we were not going to compete with machine-made products, but rather concentrate on uniqueness and quality," said Ulla.

The length and content of the training for the spinners and weavers were linked to the tasks involved and the level of expertise required. At the end of a four- to six-week training period the weavers understood the basic techniques involved and how to prepare their spinning wheels or looms. The improvement of their skills and perfection of their techniques were accomplished through daily production — the working and reworking of their products. Ulla was adamant: "We wanted absolute perfection right from the beginning. You just cannot wait for perfection at a later time, or to overcome small errors. This is something I have learnt from bitter experience."

The initial weaves were elementary in design but with experience the weavers perfected their individual skills and were able to express their talents. The first weaves tended to include only isolated figures arranged in geometric lines. Later the weavers imposed animal or human figures and positioned them on a background, so that a tapestry became a composite, and a full story was created. Often this process required the weavers to go out of the factory to study real scenes and slowly add new colours to their tapestries. All of this was done under the watchful attention of both Goweniuses, until they left in 1978.

Attention was paid to a full range of weaving skills so that each weaver was capable of high-quality production. Though no carding or washing of wool is done at the factory, for example, there was some training in hand carding so that the spinners would better appreciate the total process of preparing the wool, and, if necessary, they could do the work. The loom weavers also learned how to assemble their looms so they knew how the entire apparatus functioned.

Management Training

In addition to the production positions, there were originally five management positions that were to be rotated among workers who simultaneously held their production jobs. Positions responsible for bookkeeping, sales, wages, inventory, and raw materials were added in January 1977 after a lecture series on the various aspects of production and management. From this short course a test was given to select candidates for the five positions. Thirteen women were selected for the training for a 12-month period on a rotational basis so that each of the chosen weavers learned to work in all management positions. In this way, more than one worker became proficient in each duty. By staying close to their production duties, these individuals also maintained a direct accountability and responsibility to the workers as a whole.

The management training was shared by the Goweniuses. They

worked with individual weavers on a daily basis and as much as possible tried to make the training meaningful by linking it to actual duties and tasks. In this way they were able to identify the limited mathematical skills of some weavers and started training them in mathematics. Similarly, management committee training began when a group of women recognized that they would need specific skills to run the firm when the Goweniuses left. "Even if there were training institutions that offered appropriate skills training, I doubt we would use them anyway," said Peder. "The management skills are closely tied to the more important educational and development objectives of the project, and unless these are acquired together the training is irrelevant."

For three-month periods, the five workers holding the positions constituted the management committee (MC), each performing the duties of a conventional manager while keeping those functions ingrained in the production process. These workers were being trained as they kept the factory functioning smoothly in its day-to-day operations.

Collective Management

At the time, the MC elected a chair from one of the five position holders and this person acted as the coordinator for a designated period set by the MC. They met every two weeks to discuss the general management of the factory. Usually this consisted of reports and follow-up on former decisions. Occasionally new situations occurred, such as exhibits to plan, financial issues to deal with, or personal matters to resolve. For example, regarding personal matters, two workers were designated as mediators for worker disputes after a couple of minor incidents occurred.

All formal responsibility for decisions concerning the management of the factory lay with the MC. Anything beyond the managerial necessities of ordering materials, checking on sales or accounts, etc. — such as planning exhibitions, opening new markets, and dealing with new developments in the factory — was considered and decided upon by the committee as a whole. Issues that concerned the entire worker body — such as wages and benefits, ownership, or major changes in management policy — were taken to the full membership for their consultation and, if necessary, their decision. This was done as matters arose.

One example of how this decision-making process functioned is worth recounting. At the beginning of one month the bank balance for the factory was at a low, due to a loan repayment and delays in receiving a major overseas payment. According to Peder Gowenius this low bank balance was not overly serious because sales could make up the amount easily. However, it was an opportunity to teach and test the workers so that they would be prepared when similar crises would arise after the Goweniuses would leave the factory. The problem was discussed by the MC, who decided that everyone would lose their bonus payment for the month. In this way they could reduce the stress on the bank account while modelling how such situations could be handled by other workers.

The MC took the suggestion to the workers, who felt the reduction was too much and requested that instead a ceiling be set on wages for the month. The MC again discussed this among themselves and then proposed to the full group that working half days would be a better solution. The group suggested the idea of everyone working half a month, which they subsequently agreed on. Thus for the next month, half the workers worked the first two weeks while the second half worked only the last two weeks.

By 1979, when the workers agreed to form a cooperative, the management structure started to change. First, the Board of Directors was disbanded, ending their role in providing the overall management direction and controls. The Board had comprised representatives from the funding bodies, from the Kgatleng District (where the village of Oodi is located), and from the factory workers, along with the project managers. Second, the Department of Cooperative Development started advising and directing how some management duties should be performed. By the early 1980s major changes in management started to evolve that would lead to serious criticisms by workers and a breakdown in confidence in the MC.

A very frustrated Tidimalo Tlhagwane explained the situation this way: "The management is weak, we are just relying on this lady [Peace Corps volunteer Joan Hoff]. Things will just be the same; we'll despise each other unless someone comes to manage us. . . . This management is just staying in the office looking at the books. The members of the [management] committee don't do anything, I think they fear the manager and they don't want to admit they are not doing a proper job."

Basically, management has devolved to two main positions — manager and bookkeeper — that have been held by the same people for many years. As the training for all the members stopped and those people holding the main management positions received more training, there was less ability to rotate the positions so other weavers could gain the necessary skills and experience to manage. Therefore, one person has held the key position of manager since the late 1980s. Another weaver held the bookkeeping position until she left in 1993, and since then one member has done this work. So the workers feel there are no other weavers who can perform these management jobs, but they are dissatisfied with the performance of the people currently holding these positions.

Management duties have not been shared throughout the collective. "We didn't have any formal education and, therefore, we could not progress," says former weaver Olefile Sepotlo. "Those few with an education were on the management committee and they stayed there. Most of us without education could not do these jobs. Even if the people on the committee were unable to do the job they would still get some courses and they could stay in the job because we know even less. It would be difficult to replace them. . . . There was nothing we could do."

The MC today is largely ineffective because it is unable to manage the factory and provide the moral leadership needed. It is considered a "rubber stamp" for the manager, and many of the members of the MC feel they lack the authority and support to manage. Similarly, the full worker meetings are often unable to resolve issues after hours or days of discussion and lost production time.

As recognized in a Cooperation for Research, Development and Education (CORDE) report on the weavers in 1989,

> Oodi Weavers have an inadequate management structure, which dates from the time when the Cooperative was very much smaller. This structure has not evolved to meet new management needs as the Cooperative has developed. This means that the bulk of the membership have little or nothing to do with planning and project development. (Cooperation for Research, Development and Education 1989, 11)

Lapsed Education and Management

Peder Gowenius returned to Oodi in 1979 and 1980 for short periods to help resolve some of the administrative difficulties that had been experienced and to further train the workers in aspects of management. While the earlier visit proved productive, the second visit failed to accomplish anything, as conflict between the management committee and the other workers was starting to divide them. In 1983 the workers asked Ulla Gowenius to return to Botswana to help with quality improvements and to deal with organizational issues that continued to plague them. Her two-month stay was considered very successful and it led to a request to the Swedish International Development Agency for further production and training assistance to diversify the products being made. The proposal recommended regular short visits by the Goweniuses to maintain technical support.

Instead of agreeing to all aspects of the proposal, in 1985 SIDA supported two other Swedish weavers as occasional consultants to the Cooperative, introducing a line of woven clothing and helping with promotion. This professional advice was considered fairly productive as the product line was diversified and sales increased between 1986 and 1989. However, the weavers did not seem to adopt these changes with any lasting enthusiasm.

Broad worker education also lapsed. Weaver Tsietsi Mogapi saw the results: "When Rra Masiza [Peder] was here he was trying to train all of us about leadership so we all knew what was required of us, so we could all do the leadership positions. Ever since, though, the people in leadership don't share their knowledge with the rest of the workers, about what they are doing." There is no longer any effort to politically or socially educate the worker body since all recent member education has been provided by the Cooperative Department, which tends to concentrate only on generic instructions in cooperative regulations and requirements.

Technical training of workers since 1983 has been left largely to the weavers themselves. While they are able to pass on basic weaving skills to new workers, some of the weavers lament the lack of constant quality improvement, introduction of new skills or designs, and business skills training. Itshekeng Molwantwa, senior weaver and current chairperson of the Cooperative, identified the lacking skills: "This person [hired to train the weavers] should tell us how to improve our office business, not our weaving, not to undo and redo our weaving the way Rra Masiza did. We don't want someone to just say this cow is looking bad, we want to know why it is sick, we want someone with knowledge and who can tell us to work harder."

Cooperative Ownership

Lentswe la Oodi Producers Cooperative is a collectively owned and managed weaving "factory" or "firm." It has been designed so that only those who work in the production process have direct the control of that process. While the first objective of the project is to provide employment, it is also an attempt to keep control of that employment in the hands of the people most affected by it, through ownership and village development. In other words, ownership of the factory is not only a legal and practical function, it is a philosophical link in an ongoing process that seeks to enable people, to empower people, so they can enjoy more of the benefits of their creativity and labour.

The factory was originally registered as a public company when it was formed in 1973. This gave the project the necessary flexibility to be able to manage the many start-up requirements and to design its own ownership arrangement with the workers at the centre. Initially formal ownership was in the hands of the three financial backers of the project: Botswana Christian Council (BCC), Botswana Development Corporation (BDC), and CUSO. As members of the Board of Directors, they had partial control of the administrative and financial aspects.

Peder and Ulla Gowenius were the driving force behind starting the factory but they never legally owned the project, as was assumed by some of the weavers and people in the village. Peder and Ulla's commitment was to launch the project, train the workers, and leave the factory to the workers' collective ownership after five years, which they diligently did in 1978.

In that year the weavers started negotiations to become a formal cooperative according to the Botswana Cooperatives Act. They were not registered formally until 1981 because the Department of Cooperative Development was reluctant to register the weavers as a worker-owned cooperative. Department officials were not sure of how it should be run and organized. When registration was finally approved, it became the largest producers cooperative in Botswana and it remains so today. The workers have bought shares in the Cooperative and they are the only people able to own shares. This share ownership gives them legal authority over the entire venture. The shares earn a small interest but are only redeemable when a worker retires from the firm. Share ownership does not provide any direct income for the members.

Workers' Control

Peder Gowenius's philosophy of worker ownership was clear: "Through ownership and workers' control, the workers have the best chance to develop a cooperative spirit, a spirit of self-reliance which in my opinion is the only force capable of making this country economically independent."

Understanding and appreciating the significance of this collective ownership have taken time to develop and have not been adopted evenly by the membership. According to some of the workers not all the weavers share a similar commitment to the factory based on their ownership. As weaver Selebaleng Ndaba said, "Some have this feeling [of ownership] but others do not; I don't think they understand, even when they work they don't take their work seriously. They say, 'I don't care if the firm collapses, I only care that I have work.'"

Some of the workers, particularly those who joined the Cooperative in the 1980s and 1990s, say they do not understand all the implications of ownership. Dora Tlhagwane, one of the original weavers, pondered the question of ownership: "We sometimes wonder who really owns the firm. We bought shares and we are told we are the owners, but then the people from the Cooperatives [Department] say they can come and close us, so are they the owners? I don't know!"

Still others go beyond a conceptual definition of ownership, but question the level of authority they have. "The new members don't understand the ownership, just like some of the old ones," offered weaver Kereng Mokakangwe. "They say it is not theirs as they don't control it, nothing in it, as they don't know what is happening in the office, they don't know what is going on. Because they say they are never told how much wool is bought and how much it costs, these factors. They don't understand to what extent it is theirs."

Wages and Benefits

Wages for most of the workers in the factory are paid using a complicated formula that is based on a basic daily rate, years of service, production levels, and quality standards. This piece-rate system of wages with bonuses was intended to be fair to all the workers and to act as a teaching tool. The formula includes the following criteria:

- Because five different groups had started working at different times, there is a distinction of a few pula in their daily rate. Each worker receives a daily rate of about P8 to P12, according to when they joined the Cooperative.
- Loom weavers are also paid a piece-rate wage based on the size of the object they have woven.
- Tapestry weavers are paid a basic daily rate, but only if they reach a minimum of one square metre in a month. They are paid a production bonus if they weave more than this minimum and a sales bonus when their tapestry is sold.
- Spinners receive a wage according to the weight of the spun wool.
- Finishers, those who knot the loose ends of the tapestries and generally prepare them for sale, are paid a set monthly wage. Similarly, the persons holding the manager and the bookkeeper positions are also paid flat set rates.

Initially the different rates were designed because of the various duties in the factory and the time involved to produce different products. There was also a desire to link wages to motivation, level of output, and creative input. "With the women who had never worked before, we wanted to show that the benefits of the job were linked to their individual efforts," said Peder. "For those who had worked before, and especially those who worked in South Africa, we had to break the attitude that one tries to get the most money for the least effort. The only way of teaching this was to create a piece-rate system. When the workers are aware of the need for personal effort, then the bonuses can be dropped for a more even and equitable wage system."

Based on this system, the average wages for all the factory workers is about P120,000 a year (1996). This breaks down to an average monthly wage for all the workers of about P10,000, or up to P380 for the highest-paid worker. However, there exists a gap of about P100 between the highest and lowest wages, which is causing a great deal of resentment and interpersonal tension among the weavers. Some weavers feel all members should receive the same wage, as they all own the Cooperative equally. Others accept the need for some wage variation but they argue the difference should not be as large as it is now.

Holiday leave is for one month each year, which is usually taken in unison or at the decision of the whole worker body. Sick leave is paid in full if the worker produces a doctor's certificate, otherwise only five days in a year are paid without a certificate. For the women there is one-month paid maternity leave, though they are allowed to request three months' leave and they are encouraged to breastfeed at the factory if they want to do so. For family matters like funerals there is no limit on the length of leave but nothing is paid during these absences. However, these rules are not closely observed and are often arbitrarily applied.

To terminate employment, there must be one month's notice given by either the worker or the factory. If a worker is to be dismissed (which has not happened since the Goweniuses left Oodi), then three months' wages would be paid to cover ownership contributions. On termination, the workers receive what they paid for their shares. A gratuities program was also started so that retiring workers could get a formal pension of sorts, but this was discontinued due to low profits.

Wages, Work, and Worth

Salaries currently appear low compared to other wages paid locally and in nearby Gaborone. The government minimum wage for domestic workers, for example, is P400 a month. Other manual labour can earn about P300 to P500 a month. If a secondary school graduate can find work, s/he would start earning in the range of P700 to P800 a month, and with basic post-secondary school education or training someone can earn from P1,200 to P2,000. The starting wage for a university lecturer is about P3,500 a month or P42,000 annually.

While the wages seem to be lower than those received for other work, working in the village means fewer living expenses and other advantages that compensate for the lower salary. As former weaver Grace Ncube said, "I think I am much better off than those who work in the towns, who stay in a big house but pay rent for it. If you lose your job and you don't have a plot it will be a major problem. In my case it is better to stay at home and work in the fields and not have money, but I don't pay rent or pay for electricity or for water."

All Cooperative members have been able to significantly improve their living standards. They have built new homes with cement and metal roofing, which people in the village highly value (instead of the mud and grass thatch, for example). They have cleared or expanded their agricultural lands and provided other material support for their families.

Benefits to Workers

Mmatsela Dintwe, one of the original weavers who has left the factory, reflected a common position of many of the women when she said, "I took my children to school and my children are proud now. They say their mother worked hard and gave them something. There was nothing for me to do, I did not have work then. I also did not really have a husband as he disappeared a long time ago." Mabeleng Setswamung, a male weaver who was interviewed in 1977, said, "Life is better for me for I am working at this factory in my own village. Before I was working at the South African mines where I could not see my children and [take care of my] cattle. . . . I couldn't do anything if I was far away."

Non-financial benefits of working in the factory have been significant for the women. Many of the women reported improved relations in their families, not only for their ability to earn an income, but also because they had developed their personal skills. "The people who work at the factory have some talents even if they refuse to share those talents. Because you have been taught things, when you are with other people you'll know your rights. Someone who has not worked at the factory would find it very hard to answer your questions, because he or she will not talk to you freely like myself," reported Grace Ncube, one of the original weavers.

Another of the original weavers, Mmapala Moeng, added, "As a weaver, the main skill I learnt was to work with [other people] and how I could behave with people. Let me say that I learnt to be with people of different opinions. To deal with them depends on how you know them. I use this knowledge by being a member of the Village Development Committee and I share my ideas. When we disagree I can bring them to the right frame of mind so that we can work together, cooperate, [even though we] have a different way of talking to each other."

Benefits to the Village and Beyond

Oodi Weavers was originally designed as a development project, a venture that would directly improve village conditions and ultimately benefit Botswana society. Though it is a cooperative and is intent on improving the lives of the people who own and work in the Cooperative, it has also focused on sharing its benefits to a broader community of interest.

The most overt benefit of the project on the village is the creation of paid employment and, therefore, the measurable increase in consumer activity in the village. Currently, P10,000 to P12,000 monthly is injected into the local economy through the weavers' salaries. While some of this revenue is spent outside the village, a great deal of it is used at the local shops and bars or to pay others to work on the weavers' agricultural lands or home compounds. In the 1977 evaluation of the project, one of the most dramatic effects mentioned was the improved housing the weavers were constructing and, therefore, the overall progressive or developed impression of the village.

The chair of the Village Development Committee (VDC), Diana Meswele, said, "The firm helps the people of the village; actually it helps alleviate poverty. They don't have to go out of the village to find jobs. . . . If someone is working there they will help others who are not working, because our children are working there. Even if there is a village activity — for example, something sponsored by the VDC   they will take part in it."

In 1975, Sethunya sa Ditlhabololo (Flower of Development) was established by the factory as a small loan fund for villagers, to directly contribute to broader community development. The intent was for the factory to eventually contribute 25 per cent of its annual profits to the Sethunya fund, thus creating a growing resource for stimulating village development initiatives.

"Because we see the need for paying [relatively] high wages, competitive wages to those paid in South Africa, we create a class of workers much better off than the great majority of [people in] the village," noted Peder Gowenius. It was therefore important to channel money into the village so that others outside the factory could benefit. "It is also a matter that you are made aware that you can contribute to the development of others, to the village, and to the country. There is a social awareness in order to balance any negative effects of only backing individuals."

According to the first Sethunya trustees chairperson, Sandy Grant, the purpose of the local fund was to "lend money to production units or projects in the villages at an interest rate set by the Board of Trustees." This board was to be made up of members of the weavers' Board of Directors, four villagers, and two workers from the factory. They would then accept loan requests from individuals or groups who wanted to start production or other commercial ventures within the village catchment area of the weavers.

Sethunya lent money for a small number of projects. In the initial years, funds were borrowed to start a carpentry workshop, a "tea and bun" shop, and a small garden, and to cover some of the operating costs of a local building contractor. A butchery and a general store also received small loans. Most of these were repaid but a loan of about P1,000, taken in the late 1970s by a local businessman to start a butchery, has never been repaid. In the 1980s some of the workers also borrowed small amounts to plough their lands, much of which has not been repaid. The weavers said that if other villagers are not repaying their loans then neither should they.

The largest and most important village development spawned by the Sethunya fund was the Oodi, Modipane, and Matebele Consumers Cooperative shop. It received a loan from the fund plus a grant from the CUSO volunteers in Botswana and got off to a rousing start in 1977. It stocked food stuffs, some hardware, and building materials, all needed in the village. Because of a demand by members, the Cooperative also started to buy and sell cattle. Within a few months the Cooperative attracted almost 300 members, each of whom paid a small membership fee. For many of the villagers this shop became a source of community pride, as it was considered a major village development they initiated and operated.

The Consumers Cooperative closed its doors in 1993. After a period of doubt and suspicion about the financial viability of the shop, it closed when its manager suddenly left. According to some villagers, she and some of the Department of Cooperative Development officials had apparently pocketed about P30,000 of the Cooperative's revenues and, though given opportunities to repay the money, they were unable to do so. Members were then asked to contribute P30 each to reopen the Cooperative but caution and scepticism stopped members from agreeing to this. By 1997, after extensive discussion, the future of the Cooperative was still unresolved, though it seemed unlikely that it would reopen.

While the collapse of the Consumers Cooperative was due to corrupt management, it paralleled difficulties that cooperatives were having across Botswana. Many had collapsed, and this was attributed to low educational levels among the membership and, therefore, ineffective monitoring of the management of the Cooperatives. Corruption is widespread and hundreds of these ventures, even large profitable ones, have closed in the last five years. As part of this phenomenon, the national cooperative bodies that formerly supported cooperatives across Botswana, the Botswana Cooperative Union and the Cooperative Bank, were both virtually bankrupt and closed "until further notice" by 1996.

Today, Sethunya sa Ditlhabololo is basically inoperative, though there has been some talk among remaining trustees to revive it. Because of the limited amount of money in the fund, the failure of some key people to repay their loans, and the collapse of the Consumers Cooperative, the fund has lost its energy and has essentially been closed for the last decade. No one person has taken a strong role in maintaining the fund and, with the availability of small loan funds and grants now available from the government, some people believe that the need for such a locally sponsored fund no longer exists.

Collapse and Crisis

The profit and loss record of the Weavers Cooperative has fluctuated dramatically over the years, so it is impossible to say that the overall financial performance has been singularly positive or negative. In the early years, there was a constant and steady income growth, faster than had been expected. Statistically, growth continued over the 25 years with sales of about P50,000 in 1975; P118,000 in 1985; and P168,000 in 1995; with profits of P8,000, P36,000 and P47,000 respectively.

However, a serious "collapse," as the workers call it, occurred between 1988 and 1994, which calls into question this apparent growth in profits. During these years there was a major drop in sales, and net losses were recorded. When Joan Hoff arrived in August 1994, the situation looked desperate. "I found the management and workers at Oodi Weavers had emotionally given up hope of ever becoming fiscally stable and instead were more concerned with existing on a day-to-day basis." The entrepreneurial and management skills she brought to the firm turned the situation around dramatically.

From the perspective of one of the weavers who remained throughout the collapse, Kereng Mokakangwe, "We went through a crisis in this place but we decided to stay, to persevere, so the firm would not collapse, to help our children. Our children could progress because of the aid of this firm and that is why we are struggling with the firm."

An explanation of what went wrong, why the collapse took place, is difficult to clearly identify, as there has not been a formal evaluation of this bleak period in the weavers' history. An explanation put forward by the current manager of the Cooperative, Josephina Mokgadi, was that delays in the supply of raw materials meant the weavers used poor-quality remnants in their tapestries for a length of time. According to her, the tapestries of this period did not meet customer quality expectations and sales dropped off dramatically.

Management Deficiencies and Cooperation Problems

An external analysis of the situation in 1995, prepared at the request of the Department of Cooperative Development, indicated that there were management problems at the Cooperative and that poor planning and inadequate ordering were to blame for the collapse. According to the report by the Women's Finance House Botswana, the main organizational weaknesses were caused by a lack of

- skilful and enthusiastic management that can plan, mobilize support and implement strategies in a profitable way;
- basic business management skills among the support staff, which is causing incomplete record keeping, costing, pricing, and irregular payments;
- relevant training for the weavers, which lead to a quality and choice vacuum among the weavers and for their products;
- adequate means to produce raw materials due to late payments against credit, which in turn was caused by poor financial management capabilities among the current staff and management;

- market knowledge in relation to competition, customers' tastes, and their product affordability (Chotani 1995, 4).

However, according to some workers (and their account seems quite likely) the collapse started much earlier than 1988 and was partially due to the poor motivation and relations among the workers. As a number of weavers alleged, other weavers did not exert themselves in their work and many did not treat seriously the instructions and exhortations of the management committee. As former weaver Olifile Sepotlo put it, "The problem was that some of us were inefficient, some were not aware of what was going on in the firm. As it was, the problem could be divided into two: One, the leading committee was managing for the first time. Two, the workers who were suppose to work with them had a problem learning to work together, to cooperate, so there were some bad feelings."

This experience seemed to parallel a similar difficult period in 1982, which CORDE reported on. They noted, "The decline in sales corresponds to a period of disagreement within the Cooperative; there were conflicts between new members and founding members, and complaints about injustices. A system of equal pay replaced the bonus system which had been in force and led to a steady decline in production" (Cooperation for Research, Development and Education 1989, 4).

On the other hand, when efforts have been made to improve production and sales, often initiated by temporarily involved outsiders, there have been increases in revenue. According to Joan Hoff, when customers were engaged in conversation and encouraged to buy or if there was an improvement in weaving quality and volume, there was an immediate and observable increase in sales. "I researched many exporting possibilities [Oxfam, and others in America] and was told over and over our prices were too high. If production was increased our prices would have been more competitive. Also, without outside help [training, marketing] they would not sustain a regularly scheduled exporting project."

Overall, the instability of profits has left the Cooperative in a constantly vulnerable financial position. The weavers have not had the surplus revenue to expand facilities, attract new members, intensify marketing, or purchase new equipment. The boom and bust phenomenon has also meant that salaries have not been consistent, nor have they consistently grown, and workers have complained about this. So while it can be said that the factory is profitable overall, considering its lifespan, it is inconsistently and insufficiently profitable.

Friends of the Project

There have been a number of individuals and organizations that have offered and provided assistance to the Cooperative over the years.

Working largely behind the scenes to get the project started in the early years were people like Sandy Grant and the CUSO officials (different personnel were in Botswana between 1973 and 1986 when CUSO involvement in the project ended). They contributed their time and knowledge to help the weavers deal with numerous financial, management, marketing, and legal matters.

An evaluation of the SIDA support in 1989 indicated that much of the difficulty the Cooperative experienced was due to management deficiencies. This evaluation was prepared by CORDE of Gaborone, and they also offered to help the weavers overcome some of the management weaknesses identified in the evaluation. This offer was never taken up.

In the early 1990s, a group of interested notable people in the village, including Molebatsi Semele (who became village headman in 1991) and Ramokate Maakwe (who became district councillor in 1994), met with members of the management committee to learn about the evident difficulties the Cooperative was having and to determine if there was anything they could do to help. Informally, the Gaborone Rotary Club also offered to help the Cooperative if there was anything they could do. These offers were never taken up by the workers.

In 1993, Olaug Morse, who was living in Gaborone at the time, worked with the Cooperative as a volunteer weaver. She identified certain management weaknesses in a personal report she wrote for the Department of Cooperative Development in 1994, which led to the placing of the Peace Corps volunteer in mid-1994. During her two-year placement, Joan Hoff was able to dramatically increase production and orders for the weavers' products, which led to greater sales and much-needed income for the Cooperative. Soon after Hoff joined the Cooperative, a Japanese Overseas Cooperation volunteer Setsuko Takazawa came to the Cooperative as a design and quality advisor, and she was replaced by another Japanese volunteer in mid-1997.

On the request of Joan Hoff, an organizational analysis of the Cooperative was completed in 1995, which identified a long list of management deficiencies and made a number of recommendations for organizational and management change. This report was written by Harish Chotani, who is a member of a relatively new organization called the Small Enterprise Promotion Trust (SEPOT), which is funded by the Friedrich Ebert Foundation of Germany. SEPOT has subsequently offered to help the Cooperative with its marketing, knowledge or training, and organizational development needs.

In early 1996, local historian and writer Sandy Grant, who helped get the weavers' company started in 1973, offered to buy the factory or buildings on its land to help out the Cooperative. The offer was rejected by the weavers. On another occasion he wrote to the member of parliament and the district councillor for the area, noting the difficulties the Cooperative was going through and strongly suggesting that the government help out. In his newspaper column he wrote about the importance of the Cooperative to national development and the fact that it was not getting any government help though it rightly deserved it. "If anyone outside the project particularly cares about job creation, rural development, or any other government priority policies, they do not care sufficiently to do something about it [by helping the weavers]."

More recently, a new van was purchased with funds from SEPOT and the Friedrich Ebert Foundation, the German Development Services, and the Canada Fund (of the High Commission) — the Cooperative provided P5,000. The British High Commission paid for building renovations, the American International Women's Association replaced and repaired spinning equipment, and the U.S. Ambassador's Self-Help Fund paid for a marketing plan. Botswana Telecoms provided money for a new truck in return for permission to use a photo of a tapestry on its telephone calling card.

The most consistent support for the Cooperative has come from the Department of Cooperative Development of the Botswana Ministry of Agriculture. Since the Cooperative was registered in 1981, the Department has audited their accounts, provided general training to members in the requirements and principles of the Cooperatives Act, provided specific training to management-level personnel of the Cooperative (in bookkeeping, product costing, marketing, and stock control, for example) and, in general, offered advice on a range of issues that surfaced (e.g., the wage formula).

However, as officials of the Department were clear to point out, their role was strictly advisory and, in fact, on some occasions their advice was not accepted by the membership. The Department was responsible for requesting the American and Japanese volunteers but did so with the consent of the weavers. No direct funding has gone to the Cooperative from the Department, except for a "rescue loan" used to buy raw materials in 1993, which was still being repaid in mid-1997.

As Department officials note, Oodi Weavers is an industrial workers cooperative, which is an unusual ownership and management structure for Botswana. The Department has very little experience with, or knowledge of, this type of cooperative structure. There is currently only one other similar cooperative in Botswana: a printers cooperative in Serowe, which has not been operating as long as the weavers. The Department plans to have more specialized and knowledgeable field officers in the near future. Unfortunately, the Botswana Cooperative Bank and the Botswana Cooperative Union, two major support bodies that possibly could have helped the weavers in different ways, had both collapsed because of mismanagement and corruption by 1996. Therefore, only limited advice and support could be provided to the workers, who in some ways were more practically authoritative on the subject of workers cooperatives than anyone else in the country.

Chapter 2

The Big Picture — Goals and Background

H idden from public view are a multitude of individual and organizational actions involved in starting a cooperative or a community economic development venture. These efforts function, often unacknowledged, within a particular environment of chance opportunities and obstacles. Yet this hidden history sets the basis for what happens at the Cooperative and how people perceive what is subsequently possible or needed for it.

This chapter outlines some of the background initiative and intrigue that led to starting Oodi Weavers 25 years ago. This account of the project's history is presented to demonstrate the complexity of effort required for these ventures, and to provide an understanding of the weavers' current status. The dates, places, and names of individuals may seem esoteric, but these facts have been included to create a comprehensive account and a historical record for Botswana and, primarily, for the weavers themselves.

Ideals and Goals

Peder Gowenius had been in Botswana about six months as a consultant for Botswanacraft, the government's craft marketing agency, when he wrote the original proposal for the weaving project. At the time

(October 1972) Ulla was completing work they had started at the Rorke's Drift Arts and Crafts Centre in South Africa, where they had been located between 1962 and 1968.

The main reason for choosing weaving as the productive activity for the factory was the skill and experience of the Goweniuses. Ulla was a trained and talented weaver and Peder a professional artist and art teacher. They had started and operated two arts and crafts centres, one at Rorke's Drift and the other at Thabana Li méle in Lesotho (1968 – 1970). Another important reason for the choice was that a weaving workshop required less capital to start than other factory ideas that were considered. It could also stimulate reasonable revenues in a short time while people were still being trained. This, of course, depended on the quality of design and craft, though from the Goweniuses' previous experience, it appeared there was a good market for such hand-made products.

The objectives for the weaving project were to

- train and give employment to about 50 people in a small weaving factory;
- accumulate sufficient capital after a reasonable period of time to give employment to at least another 150 at this factory and in various smaller production units;
- keep the new wealth within the community as much as possible in order to boost local economic development and the standard of living through increased agricultural production, etc.;
- develop the experience and the knowledge received through this first project into a training programme to spread the benefits to many others.

The Project Proposal

The first phase of the project involved setting up the weaving factory. This project would employ local villagers at an average annual salary of about P200 for each worker (actual wages after three years were about P700 and today about P4,000). The anticipated sales for the factory were about P40,000 after four years of production (actual sales in 1977 were about P70,000 and in 1995 about P168,000).

The project proposal stressed the importance of "involvement in basic development at the grass roots level, to involve the people immediately concerned and of equal importance, to create a two-way response between the individuals and the community, ensuring a spirit of unity and goodwill" (Gowenius proposal 1972).

Further Village Development

The second phase of the proposed project was "to increase the involvement of and the benefits to the villagers as a whole to attempt to create a unified commitment to working towards integrated village development." This could be done by stimulating the growth of smaller production units within the three villages involved, owned by the villagers and started with loans accruing from the weaving factory profits.

The proposal explains that

> the community benefits after eight years should be considerable and should, thereafter, increase steadily. Out of a population of 1,500 people, about 20 per cent [will be] employed in the production units and another 20 per cent in seasonal production in the agricultural section. . . . It should be remembered that besides the cash return, the member as well as the community at large should and will benefit from a cooperative shop and the increased agricultural production (stimulated by the workers' direct consumption as well as agricultural production units).

Gowenius noted, "We wanted the benefits of this project to be educational as well as economical. The two types of benefits are clearly related, of course, but initially we expected people to request and work towards the economic benefits because these answered their most obvious needs; but later on when they become aware of their potential, they would start to raise questions like: what is good and of value in our traditional society, or what should we keep and what do we have to change to develop our nation?

"We did not intend to break down or to change the traditional society of Botswana, but it would start a dialogue which might help this society to change and adapt itself to the needs and requirements of a changing world."

Expanded Development

The third phase of the project was to spread the experience of the initial village to other villages, or replicate the project. According to Peder, "The main aim of this project was not to just make one village 'happy,' but to create a model for development and spread this into as many villages as possible who request it. I had no doubts that, if the community in the first village understood the far-reaching benefits of this project and as the word spread, we would have no difficulty in finding suitable teachers, suitable capital-accumulating factory ideas, and the capital required to answer requests from other interested villages." The project would spread, partially because of a reputation built on a "success story" in the first village. Gowenius proposed that technical expatriates with extensive experience in production would come to the factory before going to other production projects in the country. They would be briefed on the various aspects of the project's objectives and the specific means to those objectives, such as worker control of the enterprise.

The proposal continued,

> the number of villages in which this development programme can be extended depends of course on factors such as consumer demand, local resources, and village interest. The crucial factor seems to be the recruiting and the training of the expatriate teachers required. Not only does this project require teachers with the skill and technical experience but also sensitive people who wish to learn more and who can communicate.

Selling the Idea

In late 1972, the project proposal was sent to the Ministries of Finance and Development Planning, Commerce and Industry, and Local Government and Lands (now the Ministry of Local Government, Lands and Housing), and to the district councils of Kweneng, Ngwaketse, and Kgatleng. None of these bodies acknowledged the proposal for at least four months. The Kgatleng District was the first to respond, in a letter to the Ministry of Local Government and Lands, saying that they thought the project was valuable for rural development and that it should be supported.

When the proposal did not stimulate further reactions, Sandy Grant, then development organizer with the Botswana Christian Council (BCC) and a member of the Kgatleng District Development Committee (DDC), started to promote the proposal at the district level. Informally he arranged meetings to discuss the project and to introduce Gowenius to Kgatleng District officials in Mochudi and others in Gaborone.

In his capacity with BCC, Grant explained that there were relatively few rural development project ideas in the country and that the BCC was attempting to direct more of its support to district councils. He scrutinized and promoted projects on their individual merits and according to broad BCC guidelines. It was largely his confidence in Peder Gowenius that drew him to support the factory project. "Ultimately one had to decide whether to support or not to support [a project]. In this case, Gowenius had the skills, the experience, and the commitment to Africa. . . . It stood to reason, that any country in this sort of underdeveloped state should react quickly when presented with the opportunity of using someone of Peder's particular caliber. They are rare birds."

Grant said in 1973 that "this was another of these one-man shows, and projects of this kind obviously have a built-in weakness, but there is only a limited amount one can do about it. . . . It was worth the gamble. He did, however, have one advantage over most of the one-man type projects, mainly that he had a wife who is the weaving technician, whereas he himself is the graphic man, the communicator, and business administrator. This sort of combination was fairly strong."

Grant introduced the project to other people like Chief Lenchwe II of the Bakgatla and John Speed, District Officer, Development (DOD) for Kgatleng, who were to become instrumental in the project's inception. Chief Lenchwe was able to use his political influence to support the project, while Speed had access to the mechanisms of the government bureaucracy, which he put to use.

According to Chief Lenchwe, "I saw this project would give employment, but more important I thought the factory idea would teach people how to develop themselves, give them knowledge to do things for themselves and their village. I knew the people in government were making it very difficult for Gowenius, but we pushed for the project and got it through, because we wanted the benefits for the village.

"My only worry about the project in the beginning was if Gowenius would have the patience to keep working for the project, with all the negative reactions and cold shoulders from government. Once there was the approval and the funding I had total confidence in the project. I felt Gowenius knew what he was talking about and knew what he could do."

Speed rewrote Gowenius's proposal so it would fit the DDC format and presented the project to both the district council and the DDC, which then took up the project with the Ministry of Local Government and Lands. The reaction in the district was positive but not enthusiastic at first. The then district commissioner and DDC chairperson, Mr. Lebane, said the project "was quite complicated and I don't think it was fully understood." The project was discussed at length and, once Gowenius personally explained aspects of the project, such as funding sources, the idea of worker ownership, and the training scheme, the council "gave it total blessing. We wanted projects that were going to train our people, give them jobs, and we wanted these small projects in the small villages, not just Mochudi," said Lebane.

The discussions in the Kgatleng took place in March 1973. But it was believed that nothing could go past the talking stage until there was central government approval. Chief Lenchwe was more confident than most that the project would be approved, because "with my support, the government could not refuse. They wanted this constituency [in the elections in 1974] and would not ignore our interests."

More Selling — Getting the Project Off the Ground

Once there was formal central approval, then other government mechanisms could be set in motion, such as the provision of water for the factory, said Speed. There were other rural projects in the making at the time, and if these resources could be used, the provision of services would be possible, he added.

In the meantime, Grant chauffeured Gowenius around the district in search of a suitable location for the factory. Meetings were also arranged between Gowenius and the Botswana Development Corporation (BDC), which was a potential funding source. Paul Hinchey of the BDC said, "Our first reaction to the project was positive but guarded. We thought it would be only marginally profitable, but that if it was larger, say employing 200 or 300 people, it could be more economically attractive."

Because employment was a high priority in BDC-funded projects, Hinchey asked Gowenius to recost the project (a normal request in such consideration) and to include more people. Gowenius rewrote the projections and maintained that his original size was the most economic, and he insisted on keeping the factory relatively small. "BDC's criteria was that the project be economically viable and that it would provide employment to 50 or 60 people," said Hinchey. "Our main concern was that it would be self-sustaining."

Another person involved in getting the project off the ground was the local director of CUSO, Helmut Kuhn, who actively encouraged Gowenius to write the proposal and assisted him with the various correspondence that followed. His interest was mainly personal at first, for he needed government approval for the project as well as finance from his head office in Canada before he could use his CUSO position to support the proposal. After approval of the project proposal was granted, he was instrumental in drafting the extensive legal documents to form the weaving company.

CUSO's interest was to support a project that "wasn't an ordinary local handicrafts project," according to Kuhn. Though supportive of the immediate benefits, such as employment, it was the second phase of the project that was considered as important, that is, that the project would supply inputs which would allow the people of the villages to develop their villages themselves in the future. . . . Replicability of the weaving factory is not essential to the project, rather it is the replicability of the concepts of high quality technical and management training, disciplined business procedures, low-level expatriate input, worker ownership, village development tax [levy] and the spin-off projects that is essential. . . . Our relation to the project should be such as to promote these objectives. (CUSO 1987)

In central government the reaction to the project proposal was mixed. It ranged from "too grandiose but worth a try" to "a talent which could benefit this country but lack of initiative on the part of government could lose Gowenius." As noted by Speed, "In a way, it was understandable that there was scepticism and hesitation in Gaborone. . . . What would your response be if someone came up to you with a project to build a cooperative factory as a basis for village development with the sort of ideals that motivates Peder?"

Speed further commented: "Rural industries were not a notable success in Botswana and there were plenty of people about with wild ideas that were not feasible. It was easy to put Peder's into that category. A great deal rested on the Goweniuses to actually do what they have done, and many others would have failed with the same project.

"For an overworked bureaucrat and possibly an unimaginative one at that, it is not easy to decide to give this one a push. For a planner like a DOD who has so much freedom to play hunches, it is much easier to accept the exotic and to follow it up. When I started to push the project, I did it because I thought Gowenius was more convincing than many of the people who used to come through the office with bright ideas, but I did not think there was much chance of getting the thing through."

The government official with responsibility for approving the project was the Commissioner of Commerce and Industry G. A. Major. In letters to the permanent secretary, Ministry of Finance and Development Planning, he supported the project in concept but carefully and at length challenged the economic viability as written by Gowenius. He questioned the exclusion of a vehicle, insurance, and teacher counterparts to Peder or Ulla. He also thought some costings were too conservative. He suggested that the factory should be formed as a limited liability company and that it should be placed under the overall supervision of the Botswana Enterprises Development Company Limited (a financing branch of the then Ministry of Commerce, Industry and Water Affairs, and directly under Major's control).

He wrote,

> My experiences of "mixed motive" projects (i.e., projects which purport to link social and economic development) and which type of project I have seen attempted in more than a dozen developing countries, have led me towards an antipathy for such projects. Failures to produce the expected levels of social development are excused by the requirements to operate commercially whilst failures in commercial viability are excused by the needs to provide social service.
>
> I am strongly in favour of a well conceived project in Botswana for the development of handloom weaving. . . . If Mr. Gowenius or any other person will come forward with a well set out proposal for a handloom weaving factory, I will give such a proposal every support. (Major letter 1973)

P. Landell-Mills, then director of economic affairs, Ministry of Finance and Development Planning, also wrote to Peder.

> As you are aware, there have been a number of schemes in the field of handicraft Brigades [that provide training and employment opportunities to the local community] which have been initiated by a small group of dedicated expatriates but which have for one reason or another collapsed, leaving the government to pick up the pieces. It, therefore, is desirable from all points of view for new schemes to be very carefully planned so that one can be reasonably confident that they will be viable in all respects.
>
> In preparing the above you should know that it is our view that handicrafts training and production activities should be clearly differentiated from any ancillary community development activities. Furthermore it is most important that your scheme should be consistent with national policies concerning rural development and handicraft and vocational training and should contribute to the fulfillment of those policies. (Landell-Mills letter 1973)

A Snag in the Process

An additional problem, averted by Gowenius and his supporters, was how to deal with the official procedures of application within the government. First, there was some questioning and a challenge to Peder's letter proposal as not being a "proper and formal" request. Then there was the confusion created by overlapping responsibilities and contentious jurisdictions of the various government departments involved. These jurisdictions were coveted and guarded, and had to be managed well to get the project approved.

"My advice to John, Sandy, and Chief Lenchwe was to establish firm support for the project at district level and find independent sources of funds, then it didn't really matter what central government did," said Brian Egner, former head of the Rural Development Division in the Ministry of Local Government and Lands with direct responsibility for DDC planning activities. He believed that substantial support at the district level was sufficient to ensure donor interest, without which the project could not go ahead since it was not going to get money from Major's ministry. (That ministry controlled all government funds for industrial development.) Political factors would guarantee that central government would not bury the project, but bureaucratic opposition would ensure that it would not get any government money, he said.

"I was not going to openly support the project in central government deliberations when Major was opposing it, for he legitimately was the government expert responsible for rural industries planning and funding and our ministry had no such expertise or funds," said Egner. "Opposing Major, whose only real power was the power to deny funds to the project, would only create unnecessary confrontations in Gaborone when basically the wheels were already turning; the decisions were already being taken, in the district."

The Ministry of Local Government and Lands, through DDCs and councils, was committed to decentralization of rural development initiatives and planning, but other ministries like Commerce and Industry were strongly centralized and ruled by experts, said Egner. "I could not see where the money was going to come from. The Ministry of Local Government and Lands offered to provide P10,000 for a factory water supply under the guise of improving the village supply, but we could do nothing beyond that. The question of whether the BDC as a parastatal was truly independent of Major's ministry now became crucial."

Gowenius's Political Reputation

Ironically, what was giving Peder the edge over other potential project ideas was also the most difficult hurdle to overcome, that is, his past record in South Africa and Lesotho. Referring to rumours of Peder's political ideology, John Speed noted, "Apart from the ordinary bureaucratic problems of the government, there was undoubtedly concern at Peder's past history. . . . [A high ranking officer] specifically asked me at one stage whether I thought Peder would prove a political embarrassment." But the Rorke's Drift and Thabana Li méle centres were both considered highly successful, though the latter deteriorated substantially after the Goweniuses left. The Rorke's Drift Centre is well known today as a producer of exceptional art, and many of today's leading Black South African artists trained there at one time.

Because of these experiences, however, Peder had acquired a reputation of being potentially politically dangerous. In South Africa, the
centre was a "black spot" located in a "white area," an anomaly of the
apartheid system that created perpetual problems for the centre and the
Goweniuses. But the fact that they were able to maintain the centre for
as long as they did indicates the diplomatic skills they possessed. Peder
was eventually declared a "prohibited immigrant" by the racist South
African government for his work with the Black population. He was
also forced to leave Lesotho after the 1970 coup because of his outspo-
ken opposition to the coup and its organizers. Few people outside the
Lesotho government have disagreed with what Gowenius said, though
some have questioned his right to speak out as he did. As well, Peder
did not hide his ideological inclination towards left values.

It was partially due to the Lesotho experience that Peder felt it necessary to secure official government approval for the Oodi project
before it was started. "We did not want to be caught in the same position as with Jonathan's government [in Lesotho], when we could be
possibly thrown out of the country for what we were doing because
they did not understand the project," said Peder.

Receiving the Go-ahead

Official approval did not come until May 1973 in a letter from the
Coordinator for Rural Development, Ministry of Finance and Development Planning. By then BDC, BCC, and CUSO were well on the way
to establishing funding for the project.

"I also have to admit," said Peder, "that I did not encourage the
project as much as I could have. It was mainly other people like Sandy,
John, Helmut, and Paul who were active in getting it approved. When
I wrote the project, I was really only interested in getting my resident's permit renewed long enough to finish writing a book I was
working on. I could not do that unless I had some legitimate reason
to be in the country. After the Rorke's Drift and Thabana Li méle fac-
tories I was getting somewhat tired of weaving and wanted to do
something else. I was not totally enthusiastic about the idea and basically did not think the proposal would succeed in gaining government
approval anyway."

As the discussions progressed at the district and national government levels, Peder said he slowly became more drawn into the project,
developed more of an enthusiasm for it. When he found out that some
government officials were trying to block the project, he became more
determined to gain the approval.

According to Egner, it was Peder's idealism and his district level supporters that established the project. "I've seen dozens of similar industrial projects submitted to ministries in Botswana, which never got off the ground. The promoters didn't have the idealism and persistence that Peder and his supporters had. This idealism was necessary for they could spend the time taking the idea around to all the people concerned and they could convince others in and out of government who knew what to do next and how to do it. Finally they were dead lucky that the BDC showed its independence of Major's ministry and its risk-taking ability, thus providing at least quasi-government practical support and commitment."

It was the ability to "know what and how" — the approval process and how to access it — that finally led to political approval. After many months of discussions, the chance of official government blockage of the project appeared to have died on the desks of Gaborone officials. There was a general stalemate between Major, who wanted a strictly commercial enterprise, and Gowenius, who wanted autonomy and a mixed (socially and economically driven) project.

At this time, an exhibit of Rorke's Drift tapestries was held in Gaborone, officially opened by Vice-President Ketumile Masire (now the president of Botswana). He praised the work and expressed an interest in this type of art. He was told of the Goweniuses and the obstacles they encountered with the weaving project. At this event, key government people also met Sandy Grant and Gowenius, and this seemed to open up personal communications and rapport. Soon after came an official letter from the Ministry of Finance and Development Planning basically giving the project the go-ahead.

The approval was exactly what Gowenius wanted, though two qualifications were stipulated: (a) that a legal entity which will be responsible for the project is created, the constitution of which should be agreed with the government and the District Development Committee of the district where the project will be sited; and (b) that the project is operated within the framework of general government policy especially with regard to rural development and handicrafts.

Financing the Adventure

The money required to start the project was anticipated to be about P65,000. This was broken down into P35,000 for the building, equipment, and initial running costs of the factory and P30,000 for salaries of expatriates with the teaching and technical knowledge needed to start the factory over four years, implying that no other expatriates would work in the factory during and after this period.

Formal approval by the government was the key to releasing financial support for the project. This was BDC's first sub-commercial project loan (of R30,000 — the South African rand, at par with the pula, was the currency used at the time), and according to Hinchey, "We needed protection by government." He noted that because projects such as the weaving factory were run on a smaller profit margin and there was a perceived increased risk of failure, BDC wanted to know that the project had the general support of the government. "First there was the question of Peder's background, his Lesotho experience, and we didn't want the government to stop things if something went wrong with the project or other things changed." Second, because this was a new endeavour and in effect BDC was indirectly using public funds for the loan to support it, they wanted government approval. "By supporting the factory, we were getting a lower rate of return on our money at a greater risk. For example, we could [instead] just invest in a building society for eight-and-a-half per cent. So in effect we were subsidizing the project with public funds."

BDC considered the risk fairly high in this project. Henchey said, "Our first projections of the project's viability, or that it could be self-sustaining were not encouraging. The project appeared [only] marginally profitable, but in fact we have been proven very wrong in this case." In the event of failure, BDC felt it would not have the security it had in other projects. For example, the physical structures which would provide some compensation if reutilized could not be held as security in Oodi where there was little chance of reuse.

The dependence of the project on one manager also created the potential problem of replacement. If for some reason Peder and Ulla left the project, it would be difficult to replace them. Most sub-commercial projects depend on volunteers and it could be difficult to recruit other individuals like them, or to hire highly qualified personnel at salaries the project could handle. However, after extensive examination and a trip to Rorke's Drift, BDC did assure itself of the self-sustaining ability of the project and agreed to take the risk.

Donors for the project were confirmed shortly after government approval was received. BCC made a direct grant contribution of R10,000 to the project, part of which came from Christian Aid (U.K.) and part from Christian World Service (U.S.A.). CUSO provided R34,300; half of this came as a grant from the Canadian Catholic

Organization for Development and Peace and the other half was the CUSO salary for the Goweniuses for four years, paid in advance in one block amount. Funds were paid out to the legal body responsible for the project, the company Board of Directors. The BDC loan was not to be taken in total, but rather arrangements were made for the factory to draw out money up to the loan maximum, over three years. In fact, the factory only used R5,000 of the amount.

Limited Liability Company vs. Cooperative

Ten days after formal government approval, representatives from the ministries concerned, and from the BDC and CUSO, and officials from the Kgatleng District met with Gowenius to lay the foundation for the company that would control the project. At this meeting and at another two weeks later, it was decided to establish a limited liability company (Lentswe la Oodi Weavers Pty. Ltd.) rather than a cooperative, which appeared to be more consistent with what Peder intended for the project. A company would allow the workers to be the owners of the factory while, as Hinchey noted, "a cooperative can be owned, or the shares are bought by anyone in a cooperative and, therefore, if we wanted only the workers to own the factory, a cooperative legal structure would not do. Anyway, the Department of Cooperative Development officials would not agree to registering the factory as a cooperative because they wanted proof of success which was not possible to provide."

Location and Worker Selection

The next step in the formation of the project was to secure a location. The Kgatleng District Council had recommended either Oodi or Morwa (farther north of Gaborone), and it was up to Gowenius to select. He rejected Morwa because of the lack of water and the possible hindrance of having a major highway through the village when implementing the community development goals of the project. Oodi had an adequate water source; the population size (less than 1,000) was appropriate; and it was close enough to Gaborone for marketing, yet far enough away to maintain its identity.

However, locating the factory in Oodi depended on the agreement of the local residents. Therefore, in June a *kgotla* (village council) meeting was held in Oodi where Peder, Chief Lenchwe, Speed, the district commissioner, and a district councillor addressed the villagers of Oodi, Modipane, and Matebele. "The response was encouraging but not one of great excitement, for we didn't oversell the project deliberately in order not to raise expectations," recalls Speed. Gowenius explained the project and stressed that only about 50 people could be hired and at fairly low wages while the loans were paid off. He specifically asked for village approval of the factory to be located in Oodi and to include people from Modipane and Matebele.

Water Opens the Door to Oodi

A major factor in establishing the factory was the availability of water. At the *kgotla* meeting, the water question was raised and the people suggested reticulating water from a syndicate borehole between Oodi and Modipane. This borehole had been a problem for the district council as the "owners" had adamantly held on to it when the council was taking control of other boreholes in the district (the syndicate members had de facto ownership, for it was originally a tribal water source equipped by the syndicate). John Speed recalled that "the council and the chief saw the opportunity of resolving the dispute by taking over the borehole as part of the project. . . . I was a bit worried when the chief used his authority to decide on the matter, but it was apparently what the people wanted, to settle the matter once and for all."

With the headmen of the villages and some of the residents, a building site was also selected. Speed then made a formal application on behalf of the company to the Land Board, and allocation of the land was made in July 1972.

"Just after the *kgotla* meeting, Ulla, the boys, and I went home to Sweden," recalled Peder. "Even then I was sceptical that everything would succeed as intended; would we get the land and would CUSO come through with the money? So I made one last demand, that everything be established for us within three months or we would not come back to Botswana. Even at this late date I was not sure I wanted to do the project. It surprised me, but they did it. We came back in September and started to build."

First to be constructed was a small building in which the Goweniuses lived until their house was completed in 1974. This thatched building was then the showroom until it was destroyed by fire in 1975. The next building constructed on the site was the factory (12 metres by 28 metres) designed by Gowenius. All of the buildings were constructed by local workers and carpenters under Gowenius's supervision.

Selection of Workers

During the construction period, villagers were told application forms for employment in the factory were available from the headmen. By distributing these forms, the headmen could ensure that applicants were residents of the three villages involved. The initial response drew 170 applicants from Oodi, 60 from Matebele, and about 25 from Modipane, of which about 90 per cent were women. These applications provided a sufficient number for selection but Gowenius made another effort to solicit more interest from Modipane, which failed to generate any further applications.

The first criteria in selecting workers was their family connections. "First we tried to involve as many different families from the village as possible. Then we took people from the different families according to the numbers who applied, so that if more applied from one family they would have more workers in the factory," said Gowenius.

Peder then tried to assess their social need based on the number of children they had and how they were being supported. Gender was not used to determine workers, but the high proportion of women applicants meant a higher proportion of women were selected.

"We also tried to get at least half of the workers with a little better education, so they could provide some type of leadership to the others. We thought they should be able to understand what we were teaching better, and then could tell others. There was also the need for translation," noted Gowenius.

Based on the Goweniuses' South African experience, they tried to select middle-aged workers, for they found the older ones tended to find it harder to learn new things and to adapt to new situations, while the younger ones were too unsettled to learn well. But they did seek a range of ages so the workers would closely represent the village demography. "However," noted Gowenius, "we have found in Botswana that actually the older people, in their 40s say, are better prepared to learn. It seems the school system in Botswana prepares the younger women for urban jobs and living and they, therefore, are not as good learners in the factory."

Part of the selection process was a personal assessment by Peder. "If the person was a little cheeky, then they were more likely to question and challenge and, therefore, we selected them. Others who might be more quiet and withdrawn we preferred not to take, because it would be harder to involve them in the larger village's development goals of the project." No judgment of the person's creative ability was considered, for this was felt to be impractical.

The first group of 12 people selected for training was composed of four from each of the three villages. Other groups (eight groups of 12 were trained eventually) were composed more proportionately to the number of applications from the different villages.

On the first day of the induction, the applicants heard about the conditions of service, rules for hiring, training scheme, wages, benefits, and responsibilities of being workers. The actual training started the next day, if the applicants returned (for some did not). After the training period for each group and according to the different skills taught, the applicants were then tested. Based on the test results, the workers were selected for the factory. Those who failed were paid for the time they spent in training, while those who were successful were not paid. There was about a 75 per cent pass rate.

The successful applicants then became apprentices in the factory for one year. After this time, they were again tested and their productivity examined. If they met Peder's production standards, they were hired as factory workers. All of those who became apprentices were to become workers, though some were dismissed for low productivity within a short period.

Chapter 3

The Botswana Context

by Keitseope Nthomang

In this chapter, I shall place Oodi Weavers in the broader context of contemporary Botswana. I shall look at the people and village of Oodi from a larger historical perspective and situate the weavers in the current socio-economic and political climate that includes existing government policies and programmes. I shall also look at what the Botswana government, non-governmental organizations, and other stakeholders can do to support community economic development ventures in terms of funding, technical assistance, training, marketing, and other assistance.

For the purpose of this analysis, I am considering all Batswana as generally the same in the sense that they are a product of similar historical and economic conditions and share many common social characteristics. For another analysis it would be important to make distinctions that characterize the diversity within Batswana culture. However, for an analysis of national community economic development potential in Botswana, it is appropriate to stress the cultural commonalities and national similarities among the people rather than the differences.

Oodi Village

Oodi Weavers draws workers and support from the villages of Oodi, Modipane, and Matebele in south-eastern Botswana. This is an area of mixed settlement and agricultural land, flat acacia veldt that surrounds the booming urban area of Gaborone, Botswana's capital and largest city.

Oodi is the central village and up until the mid-1970s looked like a rather typical rural Batswana community. The village is situated on the northern slope of Lentswe la Oodi ("hill of tree bark") near the Notwane River. By a well-maintained paved road built in 1979, the village is 30 kilometres northeast of Gaborone and about 30 kilometres south of Mochudi (the Kgatleng District capital). A gravel road links Oodi with Matebele about two kilometres to the north, and a paved road to the east reaches Modipane 13 kilometres away.

When Oodi Weavers opened their doors in 1973, most villagers were occupied within an expanding form of subsistence agriculture, and though some had cattle, almost every family in the village had ploughing land. Many of these lands were and are close enough for the villagers to stay in the village during the crop season, but some people maintain two homes and travel up to 10 kilometres to their lands.

Water was first reticulated throughout the village in 1974, in part because of the factory, as water was needed for it and this was one of the conditions for placing the factory in Oodi. Seven stand pipes were installed in that year around the village. Today water is piped from a large dam near Gaborone to numerous standpipes or directly to a number of homes throughout the village.

Rapid and Extensive Change

The appearance of Oodi today is very, very different from what it was in 1973. While there is still the rural traditional village at its core, modernity has intruded in a major way. Simply put, Oodi is now a "bedroom community" or a virtual suburb of Gaborone, which, because of its own massive expansion, can now be seen from the village. The village population has increased with these changes. The 1971 population of 630 grew to about 930 in 1977, and in 1981 the population was estimated at about 1,600. The 1991 census put the population of Oodi at 2,282.

Architecturally, the round thatched huts are in the minority now as people have increasingly built more cement and metal-roofed rectangular structures. More dramatic, though, are the very large western-style homes throughout the village. Many of these are occupied by people working in Gaborone, and by the half-dozen expatriates who rent or own in the village. While goats, donkeys, and cattle still graze throughout the village they are often shaded by mature fruit trees, satellite dishes, or huge buildings like the two community centres (one privately owned and the other built by the Village Development Committee), as well as the ubiquitous acacia trees. The primary school now has modern homes for the teachers, and the Oodima Community Junior Secondary School was built in 1990 for 260 students with homes for its staff of 20.

Electricity was provided to Oodi and Modipane in the 1980s and to Matebele in 1997. While only a couple of the shops and homes have power, others use generators to provide light and to watch television (broadcast from South Africa). There are about two dozen private telephones in the village, a post office (with full-time staff, not just the twice weekly pickups of the 1970s), and a public phone booth.

The number of new residents — people not originating from Oodi — is both an asset and a liability, according to long-term residents. For example, the convoy of cars and trucks that leaves the village each morning and returns each evening provides lifts for some people who need rides (there is also a bus service that leaves Oodi hourly for Gaborone). However, these residents do not participate in village events and, therefore, are not seen as sharing in social duties. As one person said, "Some of these people, from Francistown or Zimbabwe, build here but they don't even talk to their neighbours." Or as another person said, "I like the company but they are stealing our land. They can build here and it means that I cannot!"

Business is evidently booming. While there were only a couple of shops and one bar 20 years ago, there are now six general dealers, a meat and fresh produce shop, and several bars and bottle stores, restaurants, and chibuku (a locally brewed beer) stands. Before, the only employed workers in the village were the weavers and a few government extension officers (Agriculture, Health, and Education), but now there are people working in a trucking company (with seven large lorries), a market garden and nursery, a brick-making company, a sorghum mill, and a large poultry operation (formerly owned by the Ministry of Agriculture but which has been sold to an individual who has four other similar operations). A new tribal office has been built and there is a full-time police detachment with three officers in the village. The number of people now earning a wage, either in the village or from employment in Gaborone, is significant enough that most of the shops remain open longer at night at the end of each month when people have more money to spend.

In short, the small village that was the original home to Oodi Weavers has dramatically changed economically and physically, while the personal needs of many of its original residents have remained much the same.

Physical Characteristics of Botswana

The Republic of Botswana, approximately 582,000 square kilometres in size, lies in the centre of the Southern African Plateau at a mean altitude of 1,000 metres above sea level. It is bound by the Republic of South Africa, Namibia, Zambia, and Zimbabwe.

The climate of Botswana is semi-arid. Temperatures reach 35 to 40 degrees Celsius in summer but can be very low during winter nights, often reaching sub-zero levels. Rainfall is erratic and unevenly distributed, ranging from an annual amount of 250 millimetres in the southwest to 710 millimetres in the northeast, with over 90 per cent of the rain falling in the summer months between November and April. Drought frequently occurs across the country. A severe drought from 1982 to 1988, for example, resulted in a serious decline in agricultural production and farm income.

The country lacks perennial surface water, except in the northwest where the Okavango Delta is found and in smaller amounts in the east. The availability of water has been a dominant influence on the patterns of human settlement in Botswana. The majority of the population lives in the eastern part of the country, which has reasonably good soils and rainfall in most years to produce good pasturage and to permit arable agriculture based on sorghum, maize, millet, and beans. The semi-arid climate limits the arable land to less than five per cent of the total land area, and is a serious constraint on agricultural production.

Botswana is one of the most sparsely populated countries in the world, with a total population of 1,478,000 (est. 1996), which means a population density of less than one person per square kilometre in many areas of the west. Despite its small size, the population of Botswana is growing quite rapidly, and projections for the late 1990s suggest that almost half of the population will be under 15 years of age.

History of the People

Anthropological evidence dates human existence in the area that is now Botswana back 40,000 years. However, movements of people in the 16th and 17th centuries from East Africa deposited many small groups in this area who are now the ancestors of the present-day Batswana tribes.

The Kgatleng District of southeast Botswana, where Matebele, Oodi, and Modipane villages are found, was settled with permanent residents about the middle of the 19th century. The various tribal groups — Batlokwa, Bakgatla, Kalanga, and Bamalete — were shuffled about in major migrations that settled most of Botswana as it is known today. The northward trek of the Boers after 1835 from Cape Province to the Transvaal seems to be a main precipitant of the Black migrations.

Modipane appears to have been first settled by a group of Batlokwa after their break with the Bakwena in the second half of the 19th century. They were related to the original Batlokwa, who settled in the area around Tlokweng (to the south). During the 1880s there were also a group of Bamalete who came north to Modipane from the Ramoutswa area. It is not clear why the Bamalete left Ramoutswa but they asked Chief Linchwe I (1874-1920) for permission to settle in the Bakgatla territory and were granted it. These people were led by the grandfather of the present Oodi headman, Chief Ramotudi Mokgosi.

In 1903 the largest and most permanent settlement of Oodi took place with a large migration of the former Batlokwa from Modipane led by Chief Linchwe. He thought it unwise to have a very large village located so close to the South African Boers, whom he considered a threat. The group, made up of three Semele families — Taukobong, Mochine, and Nape — moved en masse to the present site of Oodi village. They left behind the Bamalete and a smaller group of Batlokwa led by a Moeng, some of whom later came to settle in the Oodi/Matebele area.

As they were travelling to their new home, they met a group of Bahurutshe who were leaving Oodi. This group of people were returning to their traditional tribal capital at Suping in the Transvaal. They were apparently the first residents of the Oodi area and possibly were descendants of the original Bahurutshe tribe that migrated from East Africa and spawned the modern Hurutse, Tlokwa, Kgatla, and Kwena (which later broke into the Ngwaketse, Ngwato, and Tawana) tribes.

When the Modipane Batlokwa arrived in Oodi, there was already an established community of Kalanga from the north who had arrived there about 20 years earlier with the Bahurutshe. They had originally been forced south by the conflict and subsequent regional migrations caused by charismatic Chief Mzilikazi and the Zulus in the 1820s and 1830s.

The First Europeans

The first Europeans to arrive in Botswana, around 1820, were members of the London Missionary Society, the most famous of which was Dr. David Livingstone. By the mid-19th century, they had converted many of the chiefs, who ordered their people to adopt Christianity; and there were strong similarities between Christianity and existing religious beliefs of the indigenous people. British and Afrikaner merchants also set up trading posts in remote areas of the interior and would barter manufactured goods for local cattle. However, the local tribal leaders were concerned about Afrikaner encroachment from South Africa and they appealed to the British government for protection in 1872.

As Stephen McCarthy notes,

> During the latter half of the nineteenth century both eastern and southern Africa were in political turmoil. The eight major Tswana societies, within the area of what is now Botswana, found themselves threatened by the Boers, groups of whom were pushing up from the south, trying to escape British rule in the Cape. During this time the Tswana chiefs, advised by missionaries among them, repeatedly asked the British government for protection. This at least is the conventional view, though some modern scholars question whether the Tswana chiefs were quite so enthusiastic for British interference. (McCarthy 1994, 229)

By 1884, the area was claimed by Queen Victoria, and the British Protectorate of Bechuanaland was established by colonial right. However, British administration was to be limited since there seemed to be virtually no economic benefit and only limited strategic value in controlling this area of Southern Africa. Local responsibility for social and legal affairs was left with headmen and chiefs, who seemed to find the British rule acceptable, though their traditional authority was reduced.

In 1960 the first constitution was approved without the conflict that characterized independent struggles in other parts of Africa. This constitution replaced the colonial advisory council with a legislative council answerable to the British-appointed resident commissioner. The first general election to a legislative assembly was in 1965, when Seretse Khama and the Bechuanaland Democratic Party won 80 per cent of the vote. The next year the name of the country was changed to the Republic of Botswana when it became independent.

Socio-economic Context

When Botswana gained independence, after 80 years as a British protectorate, it was one of the poorest and least developed countries in the world. It had an average annual per capita income of approximately US$540 and most of the population depended on subsistence farming. The country was still dependent on Britain to meet more than half of its recurrent budget, and there was no administrative capital city. Most of the people were illiterate, and there were only a handful of university and high school graduates and just 80 students in the fifth year of secondary school (Harvey and Lewis 1990).

Almost three decades later, Botswana boasts the fastest-growing economy in the world, and the per capita income was estimated at P2,700 during 1993 to 1994. This has been largely possible due to the discovery of large deposits of diamonds, favourable world diamond markets, sound economic management, and political stability. It is important to note that Botswana's rapid and sustained economic growth has also continued in part because of considerable foreign aid since the 1970s (Duncan, Jefferis and Molutsi 1994). And in a broader-based analysis McCarthy writes, "Much of Botswana's success can be attributed to its particular historical circumstances — an ethnically homogeneous society, an apparent tradition of legalism and constitutionalism, and a continuity between the pre-colonial order and the modern nation state" (McCarthy 1994, 238).

Between 1966 and 1995, Botswana's real GNP per capita grew at an average annual rate of six per cent, which was the highest of any country in the world. Over the same period, formal sector employment increased at an average annual rate of nine per cent. By 1995, with a GDP per capita of US$2,850, Botswana was one of the few African countries to have graduated from the least developed to the middle income group of developing countries (Duncan, Jefferis, and Molutsi 1994).

Proportionately, Botswana also has the largest foreign currency reserves in the world and could wipe out its foreign debt at the stroke of a pen, still leaving enough cash savings for a full annual budget (Hedenquist 1992). Currently Botswana's foreign reserves stand at about P20 billion.

An impressive aspect of Botswana's rapid economic change has been its social gains, as indicated by significant improvements in key social indicators. Between 1970 and 1990, under-five mortality and infant mortality rates were halved and life expectancy at birth rose from

46 to 65 years for both genders. In 1990, 86 per cent of the population had access to health services, immunization of children stood at 78 per cent, about 90 per cent of the population had access to safe water, and 55 per cent had access to sanitary facilities (Government of Botswana/UNICEF/UNDP 1993). Adult literacy and primary school enrollments doubled, and over 70 per cent of primary school leavers gained access to secondary schools. Females constituted half of the primary and secondary school populations.

Increases in Wage Labour

The economic growth Botswana has experienced has also created a new wage-class of people. Growth in Botswana's public sector has been a major source of jobs, and over 30 years this growth has resulted in a large urbanized bureaucracy. Private sector job growth has also grown significantly, changing the income distribution for all Batswana. As Charles Harvey noted, "The remarkable growth of formal sector employment in Botswana since Independence is arguably the most important way in which the benefits of rapid growth have improved the distribution of income" (Harvey 1992, 15).

According to a Bank of Botswana report,

> Growth in job opportunities averaged about 10% per annum over a 30-year period and transformed the structure of the economy from one in which 90% of the labour force were formally engaged in (mainly subsistence) agriculture . . . to one in which less than 20% of the labour force are engaged in agriculture. Thus whereas 10% of the labour force was in formal employment in 1966, the same ratio was nearly 50% in 1991. (Bank of Botswana 1996, 22, 61–69)

The report goes on to note,

> At an individual level, formal sector employment is important for the higher income it provides and the human dignity it bestows as well as greater impact on raising the quality of life. As a result of economic growth, household consumption expenditure has increased in real terms between 1985/86 and 1993/94 according to the Household Income and Expenditure Survey (HIES). For example, in urban towns the average monthly expenditure was P1,258, compared to P672 and P392 in urban villages and rural areas respectively. The national average stood at P716 compared to P197 in 1985/86.

Wealth and Poverty

The Bank of Botswana further observed, however, that "the growth in employment opportunities was insufficient to absorb all members of the labour force who wanted formal sector jobs. Thus while formal sector employment growth was large enough to absorb the growth in the labour force, it was not large enough to absorb all those Batswana who sought to leave the agricultural sector."

In Botswana the economic boom has thus resulted in high-income groups possessing more income-generating assets (i.e., productive assets, human assets, or both), and they are in a better position to benefit from increased national income. R. L. Curry concluded that inequality in Botswana has increased significantly due to what he saw as a declining rural household income and unequal income distribution (Curry 1987). He attributes this inequality to structural imbalances in the economy, government policy choices, inequality in asset ownership, land use, and water rights, and unequal access to wage employment opportunities.

Therefore, despite the impressive development statistics, there is persistent poverty, unemployment, and income inequality, particularly among women and youth in Botswana. Uneven distribution of income exists, and benefits of the growth windfall have not sufficiently trickled down to all groups in society, as only a small proportion of the people (cattle owners and high-wage earners, in both the public and private sectors) have benefited from Botswana's economic development.

Clearly, the unemployed, the urban and rural poor, and the population dependent on subsistence farming have not experienced benefits comparable to what wage earners have experienced. Estimates obtained from the 1985/86 Household Income and Expenditure Survey indicate that 55 per cent of the rural households were living below the poverty datum line (PDL). Conclusions of the Rural Income Distribution Survey of 1974/75 also revealed that about 45 per cent of the rural households had incomes below the rural PDL, and by 1985/86 the figure rose to 64 per cent (Government of Botswana, Central Statistics Office, 1991). The situation remains relatively unchanged today, as shown by a poverty study conducted by the Botswana Institute for Development Policy Analysis (1997). The study reveals that poverty levels in Botswana are increasing rather than decreasing, with more than half of the population living below the PDL.

Income levels are considerably lower among female-headed households. Nearly 40 per cent of women earned less than P100 per month in cash and in-kind income compared to about 25 per cent of men. According to the Policy on Women (Government of Botswana 1995) female-headed households, which constitute about 47 per cent of all households, have to survive on the lowest incomes while having to meet additional burdens of bringing up children and attending to other family responsibilities. This situation places enormous responsibilities on women as sole breadwinners and care providers, and has serious adverse implications for a range of issues from national productivity to child development.

Since Batswana men are generally better educated than women, their unemployment rates are lower. However, recent studies have shown that the number of educated women is increasing in the work-force but at rates that suggest Botswana women are still encountering other barriers to labour force entry. Also, compared to men, women who are employed have much lower representation in the formal sector and greater representation in the informal sector (Jefferis 1993), a trend that is consistent with findings for developing countries generally.

Duncan, Jefferis, and Molutsi (1994) have shown that despite increased expenditure in such sectors as health, education, housing, and others related to social development, poverty has remained a persistent condition for a substantial proportion of the population. They attribute this anomaly to harsh climatic conditions, low variable agricultural pro-duction, lack of employment opportunities and appropriate skills, and limited access to such productive assets as cattle, draught power, water, productive land, and credit. The report by the Government of Botswana, UNICEF, and UNDP (1993) maintains that despite the general improvement in the quality of life in Botswana, poverty is still a major social problem.

The Socio-economic Impact of HIV/AIDS

Botswana has one of the highest rates of HIV infection in Africa. Since the first case of AIDS was diagnosed in 1985, the virus has assumed epidemic proportions. Data collected since 1992 show that of Botswana's population of 1.5 million people, more than 14 per cent have been infected with the virus. Based on the current spread rate, it is projected that by the year 2000 there will be 332,000 people infected (Government of Botswana Human Development Report 1997).

Revised estimates of Botswana's mortality rate and life expectancy, after adjustments for the projected impact of HIV/AIDS, indicate that Botswana's life expectancy will fall from 67 to 52 years at the turn of the century, plummeting to 33 by the year 2010.

The BHDR report's analysis of the contributory factors that have led to the rapid spread of HIV/AIDS in Botswana, include:

- high mobility of the population, partly because of the tradition of having several homes (i.e., village, lands, cattle-posts, etc.). Botswana's good transport and communication systems have also facilitated this movement;
- high rate of urbanization, which has led to the erosion of traditional safeguards for controlling sexual and social behaviour;
- poverty and gender biases, which often disadvantage and subordinate the poor and females in sexual and social relations; and
- multiple sexual partners and the frequent change of partners.

It is now becoming clear that HIV/AIDS is having substantial economic and social impact on individuals and on the society at large. According to the BHDR report, HIV/AIDS is now the most serious threat to human development in Botswana. The fact that 25 per cent of men and women aged from 15 to 49 years are infected has implications for the economic well-being of families, since these people are the most economically active sector of the population. By the year 2000, it is expected that over 65,000 children below the age of 15 years will be orphaned.

Evidence suggests that women are the worst hit by the epidemic in Botswana. About 55 per cent of the reported AIDS cases in 1996 were females aged between 20 and 29. Given that women are generally the poor in Botswana society and that women head 45 per cent of the households, HIV/AIDS is likely to have severe social and economic impact beyond those directly infected (Barnett and Blaikie 1992).

According to Aggleton and Bertozzi, for a household that has lost a mother, there is a statistically significant reduction in the number of hours children spend at school, especially children aged between 15 and 19 years. The number of child-headed households increases as adult family members are lost to AIDS. Furthermore, child labour increases as the number of economically active adults decreases (Aggleton and Bertozzi 1995).

Orphaned children will obviously place additional stress on communities and caring mechanisms. Many children who are orphaned will, as a result, become very poor, and some are turning to the streets as prostitutes or criminals. HIV/AIDS is, therefore, creating another crisis of a lost generation of children, shunned, stigmatized, and abused by society (Government of Botswana Human Development Report 1997).

Health facilities are collapsing under the strain of HIV/AIDS. According to the BHDR (1997), seven out of every ten beds at Nyangabwe Hospital in Francistown are occupied by HIV/AIDS patients, while half of all beds in Princess Marina Hospital in Gaborone are occupied by patients with HIV/AIDS-related diseases.

Higher adult mortality is also depleting the formal labour force and reducing the quality of trained workers. Many workers die or need to care for a sick relative. Worker debt is increasing as families stretch their limited budgets, sometimes needing loans to meet medical costs and funeral expenses. The problems of lost working hours, high labour costs, and additional training are already being felt.

Government Policy

The formulation of public policies and programmes in Botswana are guided by four national principles: democracy, unity, development, and self-reliance. These principles form the cornerstone of the country's official development direction. They are rooted in the traditional culture of Botswana, and when applied together in practice are suppose to achieve *kagisano*, or social harmony. On these national principles the government has based its planning objectives and development strategy, which focus on rapid economic growth, social justice, economic independence, and sustained development. Hedenquist observes that

> the planning objectives and related policy statements form together the development strategy of Botswana. The ultimate goal of Botswana development strategy is thus . . . to improve living standards of all Batswana and achieve social justice, with priority given to the rural areas. (Hedenquist 1992, 60)

This goal has been revised and refined in successive national development plans, but it remains the basis of the country's policies, programmes, and institutions within which social development has been planned and implemented. In simple terms, all development activities in Botswana are guided and informed by these general principles, and this takes place within a democratic framework.

Does CED Fit with the Policy?

Community economic development, as a formal development strategy and terminology, is not used in Botswana government planning, as there is no formal policy on CED. In practice, CED (as defined in this book) is similar to the concept of "community revitalization," which functions within and has largely been influenced by the guiding principles that form the basis of all central government structures. This concept is based on

(a) designing and implementing policies on rural development, water supply, education, and health services across the country in an equitable way; most importantly, these activities can be carried out through the spirit of self-help (*ipelegeng*);

(b) channelling national and foreign resources towards the most needy sections of the populations, such as urban squatters, the rural destitute, and the Basarwa (San/Bushmen); and

(c) overseeing the management of resources and the accountability of institutions.

As reflected in a major report by the Botswana Institute of Development Policy Analysis (BIDPA), rural revitalization can occur when

> long term poverty alleviation is integrally linked to people's access to sustainable income-earning opportunities, whether through employment or self-employment. Ensuring that access is widespread is one of the key problems facing many developing countries. Such countries are often constrained by high population growth rates, small and undiversified domestic economic structures, and a lack of infrastructure, skills and financial resources. Policy interventions to each such constraints can potentially have an important impact on income and employment growth, and hence on reducing poverty, but it is essential that such policies are appropriately designed. (Botswana Institute of Development Policy Analysis 1997, 89–91)

National and Local Government Structure

Botswana has established a fairly comprehensive institutional framework for supporting general development. The governmental structures and institutions in place create a strong, partly decentralized system of administration, which can accommodate other development partners, such as NGOs and community-based organizations. Botswana's extensive infrastructure of local government institutions has been of central importance to local development efforts in Botswana. Towns and district councils in particular have been charged with the responsibility of providing a variety of social services, such as education, health, water, and various aspects of rural development like drought relief and labour-based projects.

However, this institutional framework of local government has largely ignored village economic development and other directed activities that can discover sustained solutions to the problems of rural poverty and unemployment. There was virtually no mention of the word "economic" in relation to the creation and building of community-based committees and structures during the first decade after independence, for example. There were a few uncoordinated efforts at the local level, but they did not get support from the government in terms of either human or financial resources. This was not surprising at the time, and to some extent now, since neo-conservative thinking has dominated the economic development agenda of Botswana.

In Botswana, the government's main approach has been to promote large-scale commercial growth on the assumption that reinvesting the returns from the broader economy will create other productive assets to sustain smaller, specific income-generating activities throughout the country. The assumption is that urban economic growth will trickle down to other sectors of the economy and more people will benefit in terms of jobs and an improvement in the standard of living.

An example of this approach to development is the Integrated Field Service programme in the Ministry of Commerce and Industry. This programme has different components, such as the Financial Assistance Policy, which is an attempt to develop job creation opportunities by promoting locally based individual businesses. The major limitation of this policy is that it focuses on individual entrepreneurs and privately owned businesses, without any attempt to extend and adapt the programme to community-based organizations.

Community and Supporting Organizations

The country's institutional infrastructure retains strong centralized tendencies, with lesser responsibilities for local government and a comparatively small role for NGOs and community-level organizations. Members of the local communities have virtually no real direct input into development policies and programmes that affect them, since little has been done to build institutional capacity at village or community levels.

Policy initiatives are transmitted in a top-down manner, and they often take the form of directives that do not allow people's meaningful participation in their formulation. The people are, however, expected to become involved in the implementation process, whether they agree with it or not (Harvey and Lewis 1990). Therefore, it is difficult to translate policies into reality. Despite Botswana's democratic traditions, the country continues with a rather bureaucratic approach to policy formation, justified on the basis of low education and literacy capacity at the rural levels, and the urgent and immediate needs of people at the grassroots level.

However, as Charles Harvey writes, there are contemporary dynamics that are creating new conditions for policy and programme development in Botswana.

> It is possible to argue that the huge backlog of neglect inherited at independence has been significantly reduced, . . . it may just be the case that the enormously expensive process of catching up with pre-independence neglect has been achieved during the period of financial surpluses, or at least before the accumulated surpluses are all spent. . . . it can be said that Botswana is starting on a new phase of development when the structure of growth will be quite different from that of the last 15 years with the economy and the government's reputation for sound policy a bit battered but fundamentally intact. (Harvey 1992, 28)

Links with NGOs

The Government of Botswana, since independence, has established a general informal framework of linkages with non-governmental organizations. These are generally foreign-owned and externally based organizations, but have nevertheless played an important role in providing funding, skills, and jobs in local communities. These constitute separate and distinct development partners for both local and central government institutions.

The input of these organizations tends to enrich the policy process as they complement government contributions and interventions. The government realizes that NGOs' contributions quite often determine the extent to which disadvantaged people (at personal, group, or community levels) can be empowered. Through collaboration, partnerships, and participation, NGOs have assisted disadvantaged groups and communities to break out of apparently helpless situations in order to effectively control their own development and, ultimately, their own destiny. At times in Africa, and elsewhere in the developing world, the absence of NGO activity simply means that there is no social development for the people (Mwansa 1995), hence the desire by government to involve such agencies in the development process.

However, difficulties arise in involving the NGOs when there is no official framework or linkages between the state and the NGOs (Farrington, Satish and Miclat-Teves 1993). In Botswana until recently (1996) there has been no overall NGO body to provide a framework for organizational cooperation with the government. The Botswana Council for Non-Governmental Organizations (BOCONGO) has recently been founded to provide a structure for NGOs to mutually cooperate with the government in various endeavours. In recognition of its potential, BOCONGO has been invited to have input into the current National Development Plan (NDP8), for example. Perhaps most importantly, BOCONGO is in a strong position to receive from its affiliates information on public policy issues and to bring them to the state at the highest level.

CED Examples

The Botswana government has always placed emphasis on rural development, and all national development plans have emphasized the need to focus on areas where the majority of the population still lives. In the first years of NDP3 (1973 to 1978), the government launched what was considered a major programme aimed at achieving visible rural development. The strategy focused on, among other things, the provision of social services and the generation of income-earning opportunities.

This emphasis in development planning was considered essential to improve the self-reliance of rural households and reduce their dependence on the government. Through concerted efforts to create employment opportunities and income-generating activities, they tried to address the issues of poverty and other inequities facing Botswana.

While there are very few examples of successful local rural development organizations, two important ones are the Kuru Development Trust in Ghanzi and the Maiteko Tshwaragano Development Trust in Zutshwa. These are Basarwa (San/Bushmen) organizations that have been very successful in meeting employment and training needs of the Basarwa (Nthomang and Rankopo 1997). These organizations have followed the CED integrated approach; that is, they have merged the local initiatives with national and international support to fight poverty and unemployment.

In the 1990s a downturn in the economic fortunes of Botswana hit the country hard. The main fuel for the economy, diamond revenues, did not grow much. Given population growth rates of 3.5 per cent per annum, the growth of real GDP per capita was expected to stagnate or even decline. In the absence of new growth, the challenge for the government was to focus on efforts to diversify the economy and expand the nation's physical and human resources. In this regard, some Batswana have called for a shift in the country's development paradigm, to emphasize investment in the nation's human resources through education and better training as well as social and economic empowerment of marginal communities.

The Ministry of Finance and Development Planning report on

Community-Based Strategy for Rural Development (Government of Botswana, Ministry of Finance and Development Planning 1997), for example, is an indication that government officials recognize the problems at hand and are trying to find more effective development strategies. Community-based approaches to improve rural incomes and reduce poverty are now being considered. These strategies that enable communities, through decentralized leadership and greater public involvement in identifying needs and implementing development activities (in partnership with government, NGOs, and other actors), are now seen as potential alternatives to traditional top-down strategies.

Cooperatives and Small-scale Industries

Rural development organizations such as the cooperatives and Brigades were early initiatives employed to address rural poverty. They continue to be instrumental in meeting the needs of the rural people as they play a catalyst role for job creation and rural development in general. And despite the government's tendency towards large-scale and infrastructure development, these two organizations get significant official support.

The first cooperative society in Botswana was registered in 1964 under the Cooperative Societies Act (1962). From this beginning, the movement has shown considerable progress and has provided a substantial contribution to the economy and the general development of the local people.

The cooperative movement is one of the largest business concerns in the country, entirely owned and managed by Batswana. Cooperatives offer services that are otherwise not available to the local people, mainly the poor who live in rural and remote areas. For example, they provide livestock marketing in inaccessible areas and also provide agricultural credit for livestock inputs and agricultural implements.

In the 1960s and 1970s, there was growing interest in the cooperative movement on the part of the government and rural people. Many cooperatives — consumer, marketing, savings and credit, and production — began operating at the time. As a part of the government's development policy and strategy, cooperatives were initiated, since they were generally thought to be better able than the central government to mobilize the rural population. Cooperatives were considered closer to the people in the rural areas and, therefore, better able to adapt their services to them, to make use of resources for the benefit of the poor, and to generally be more responsive to their needs. Most importantly, they were able to inform and educate members on how best to improve their livelihoods.

The Future of Cooperatives

For NDP8, it is expected that increased emphasis will be placed on production cooperatives and the encouragement of greater commitment and cooperation among cooperative members. The government is promising a lot of support for the cooperatives: about P3 million, for example, is being allocated for the education and training of management committees. At the time when free market economics are displacing the small person from the marketplace, there is a need for direct support to ensure that cooperatives will survive, notwithstanding the challenges of competition in the free market.

In principle, cooperatives have a lot in common with CED. For example, cooperatives value self-help, self-responsibility, democracy, and equality, which are the base values of every CED venture. And cooperatives in Botswana are founded on the following principles that are also inherent in CED ventures:

- Membership is open to all persons able to use their services and willing to accept responsibility without gender, social, racial, political, or religious discrimination.
- They are controlled by members who actively participate in setting policies and making decisions. Members have equal voting rights, democratically control the capital of their cooperatives, usually receive dividends on capital subscribed, and allocate some of the surplus to reserves.
- They are autonomous self-help organizations controlled by their members.
- They provide education to their members and management committees so that they can contribute effectively to the development of their society.
- Cooperatives strengthen the cooperative movement by working together within local, national, regional, and international structures.
- Cooperatives work for sustainable development in their communities.

While these principles are admirable, many Batswana feel they are simply statements on paper and have largely been ignored by Department of Cooperative Development officials and members. Often, extension workers (social workers, veterinary assistants, agricultural demonstrators, teachers, nurses) don't have the slightest idea of what a co-op is suppose to do or be. This is a serious deficiency, for these are the people best able to spread development information throughout rural areas of the country.

The reality is that the cooperatives in Botswana are now facing major problems, including the lack of entrepreneurial skills, managerial capacity, and access to credit. There are also communication problems between co-op members, management, and boards of directors, who often delay calling meetings and informing members about issues. Another problem is that cooperatives are dominated by elderly people who are generally refusing to give way to the younger generation. These members lack confidence in younger, better-educated managers, and in many cases have exploited the illiteracy and ignorance of the members. And in some cases, people have been placed in management positions because of their political affiliation rather than by merit.

Thus, in many ways the cooperative movement does not have a vision or vibrant goal to work towards. Goals that exist have been imposed from outside, mainly by the Department of Cooperative Development, and many members tend to view their societies as a part of a government body, and not as their own. A "we/they" attitude has developed that has paralysed the co-op movement in Botswana. These difficulties have surfaced as many cooperatives experience new complexities, including the changing nature of their businesses, increased competition, and flooding of cheap goods from other neighbouring states, especially South Africa.

Training and Production Brigades

Brigades are independent, community-based organizations engaged in local development by providing training and employment opportunities and offering services to the local community. They are one of the main providers of technical and vocational training in Botswana. An important element of government development strategy is to encourage commercial and industrial development in large villages and rural areas through the activities of the Brigades.

The first Brigade (Serowe Builders) was founded in 1965 by Patrick Van Rensburg, then principal of Serowe Swaneng Hill Secondary School. He noted the large number of primary school leavers who did not get a placement in secondary school, because in those days there were many fewer schools. The education system at the time was primarily theoretical and, therefore, its benefits to the country as a whole were limited. Van Rensburg's solution was to start a centre that provided theoretical and vocational education combined with productive work. Income from the trainees' production work helped to pay for their training. It was soon realized that the Brigades were an answer to the needs of both the school leavers and the community. As a result, more Brigades were established throughout the country.

At present there are 32 Brigade centres — at least one in each district. They offer training to more than 2,600 Batswana in 14 different trades. The Brigades operate on a commercial basis. They provide manufactured goods, commercial services, and formal employment opportunities to the local community. Commercial and manufacturing activities are conducted in the areas of construction, mechanical trades, agriculture, textiles, milling, and bakeries. Some Brigades, such as the Kweneng Rural Development Association (KRDA), are involved in community development work, much of it being textile work and agricultural activity, aiming to develop the participants' self-reliance.

The government will continue to support the Brigades as defined in NDP7: "Creating income earning opportunities in the rural areas, will remain a major rural development objective during NDP7, as government will enhance the role of the Brigades by channeling funds for the development of technical, managerial and training in productive activities" (Government of Botswana NDP7 1991, 327).

Brigade education tends to support CED as it creates a better-informed and skilled rural population. The Brigades provide participants with the skills that lead to productive employment and increased rural incomes as well as self-reliance. Indirectly, through effective participation of the rural people in the social, economic, and political processes, the Brigades enable people to become partners in determining the necessary features of development. One drawback is that most of the skilled artisans do not stay and work in the rural areas where they are trained. Without the benefit of recent tracer studies on the trainees, it appears that trainees migrate to the urban areas where construction and other related industries are concentrated and are paying higher wages.

Small-scale Industry

The Government of Botswana is also supporting the development of small-scale and informal industries as another means of stimulating urban and rural development. While there is a crucial lack of Batswana with a combination of entrepreneurial skills and technical abilities, there is a definite need to create employment that is independent of the government. Small-scale and informal activity is able to provide employment for the poorer section of society, and this activity requires relatively little in terms of government resources.

Constraints often experienced by informal and small-scale business include lack of access to credit and to reasonably priced and stable sources of input supply, production and technical obstacles, bookkeeping and management deficiencies, and marketing problems. Because many of these constraints are often interlinked, the government has created integration and coordination supports. For example, coordination in the rural areas is performed by the production development committees and rural industrial officers. At a national level, the Ministry of Commerce and Industry will establish a coordination body to consider methods and priorities for filling most significant gaps in the extension network, particularly in regard to input supply and marketing, and will initiate the Integrated Field Services to encourage the establishment of all types of small enterprises in rural areas.

Stephen Lewis and Jennifer Sharpley note that slow progress in commercial development in Botswana has been due to poor planning and development supports, not the lack of will or opportunity. They point out that "the constraints to further manufacturing growth were neither the shortage of foreign exchange, nor the lack of adequate incentives for manufacturing development, but other real resource constraints: water, developed land, and skills of the citizen labour force" (Lewis and Sharpley 1988, 44).

The government is encouraging the use of local materials, and will identify production opportunities and assist Batswana small businesses to improve and expand production. For example, there is considerable scope for expansion in the handicraft industries, such as textile production and weaving. The Brigade and cooperative systems offer an excellent means of expansion in these areas at minimal cost, and of training people in rural industries, particularly in techniques of production. The government will assist cooperatives and Brigades to expand in these directions by supplying credit for working capital, plants, and equipment. Producers will be assisted through credit schemes of the National Development Bank, Botswana Craft Trust, and the cooperative movement. External assistance is also being sought.

It is important to note that Botswana's proximity to South Africa and its membership in the South African Customs Union (SACU) have both positive and negative implications on economic activities in the country. Under the SACU agreement, goods are supposed to move freely within the region. Although South African products freely enter Botswana, the same has not been true for Batswana goods as a result of South African protectionist tendencies and market barriers. For example, in April 1995 the South African government banned the duty-free importation of semi-knocked down Hyundai vehicles assembled in Botswana on the grounds that such importation threatens South African employment. The decision not only affected Hyundai Botswana but also some 30 semi-knocked operations in the SACU area (Mwansa 1995).

Moreover, Botswana membership in SACU has frustrated the development of import-competing industries, which have faced limited growth potential as a result of the rather small size of the Botswana domestic market (International Monetary Fund 1995). As a result, Botswana has been quite important to the South African economy, particularly as a protected market for its manufactured exports. Nonetheless, SACU is regarded as one of the more operational and properly functioning customs unions in Africa (Stoneman and Thompson 1992; African Development Bank 1993).

Botswana's economy is also fairly isolated from the major markets of Southern Africa, and this increases the costs of both importing inputs and getting manufactured exports to their destinations at competitive prices (African Development Bank 1993). The effect has been the emergence in Botswana of a very shallow industrial base comprising manufacturing enterprises that primarily produce a limited number of consumer-oriented products for local consumption. Also, Botswana's manufacturing enterprises are highly concentrated in the urban areas and are primarily foreign owned, despite comprehensive and commendable government policies for promoting local entrepreneurship (Government of Botswana NDP7 1991; Kaunda and Miti 1995).

The Future for CED in Botswana

It is against this background that CED in Botswana is evolving. There is a history of community-based projects and activities that can inform planners and policy makers as to what will or will not benefit rural development. A number of NGOs and a support network have been working at the community level and are venturing further into education, income-generating activities for self-employment, and community organizing for empowerment. Institutions and mechanisms for the advancement of CED have been created at local, district, and national levels since independence. And government officials seem to recognize the potential of CED (Government of Botswana, Ministry of Finance and Development Planning 1997).

However, these local, district, and national institutions and mechanisms are weak; notably, the village development committees, which should and could provide the vision and supportive framework for community-based programme strategies such as CED, are not able to do so because of various cultural and political barriers. The problems encountered in implementing community-based programmes in Botswana also point to the lack of financial, personnel, and training resources available.

Adequate budgets, resources, and professional capacity to effectively implement CED tasks are needed. To foster these requirements, it is important for the Government of Botswana to establish a clearer CED strategy that could

- strengthen local, district, and national mechanisms and bodies to take responsibility and commit themselves to CED;
- ensure that government bodies have more clearly defined mandates and the authority, resources, and competence to influence policy decisions;
- ensure reporting on a regular basis to Parliament, cabinet, and other inter-ministerial committees on progress to ensure that community concerns are in line with the implementation of the community-based programme strategy;
- ensure the formulation and implementation of CED national policies and programmes;
- promote and coordinate overall CED policy formation within the central government in order to incorporate CED in all policy making; and
- establish cooperative relationships with relevant branches of the government and with pressure groups — NGOs, women's organizations (such as Emang Basadi), and other influential actors.

Government Commitment and Formal Support

The lack of commitment and support from the national political leadership is another reason CED organizations are not functioning as well as they could. Louis A. Picard writes,

> Botswana's rural development policy continues to reflect a pattern of technocratic solutions for political problems. The country could serve as a "textbook" for the types of development policy recommended by the World Bank. Expatriates continue to play a major role in what has been a bureaucratically dominated state since 1966. Ultimately, policy makers in Botswana continue to perceive rural development as linked to a more fundamental "modernization" process that assumes a dichotomy between

the traditional and the modern economies. This assumption ignores the structural links between rural agricultural underemployment and the labor reserve system that operates throughout the southern African region. (Picard 1985, 264)

Achievements, however small, can easily be identified and consolidated if the political will and policy supports are clearly expressed. It is, therefore, important that the government come up with a clear policy on CED and that this be included in the current plan period (NDP8). This policy clarification will go a long way towards assisting different stakeholders involved in addressing problems of marginalized communities.

For existing resources and mechanisms to function effectively, a national body is also needed to promote and coordinate CED. Placed at the highest level, possibly in the office of the president, there should be a senior and powerful office to influence policy direction and other ministries in support of CED. It would be important for this body to designate a senior officer to work in a coordinated fashion to ensure CED activities are implemented within the established structures. A central policy review committee could be established to monitor and evaluate CED activities at national, district, and local levels.

Equally important is the need to take advantage of existing policies that set out parameters for CED, for example, the "Community-Based Strategy for Rural Development 1997," which has set the stage for CED in Botswana. As indicated earlier, the purpose of CBSRD 1997 is to expand rural economic activities and reduce poverty. It also recognizes that existing institutional arrangements offer communities little opportunity to take part in shaping the approach to rural development activities, and this has undermined community leadership structures and contributed to a syndrome of dependency on the government. CBSRD 1997 should be seen in the light of current economic trends, especially government policy on privatization.

Taken together, the above measures could stimulate the integration of CED thinking and practice into legislation, public policies, and programmes in Botswana. Integration can be more effective in confronting rural underdevelopment than are the disjointed efforts currently in place. Experience since independence — when the government started to improve the socio-economic conditions of rural communities — shows that, without a clear policy direction, bits and pieces of activity that would otherwise be positive are ultimately of little consequence.

For CED in Botswana to be successful, specific activities have to be supported by appropriate policies and government programmes. CED organizations and ventures, like the Oodi Weavers Cooperative, cannot operate in a vacuum or in isolation. In order to attain their goals of addressing poverty and unemployment, these CED groups have to be engaged in a wide range of economic and social justice activities, independently and through alliances with organizations of similar interest (Shragge 1997). To allow the variety of resources to flow and activities to operate effectively, CED practitioners and practice need supportive relations and a broad nurturing environment, which somewhat exist in Botswana, but not to the extent needed to help the poor towards self-reliance.

Part 2

The Analysis

Chapter *4*

Participant Evaluation 1977

For six months, early in 1977, the workers took part in an evaluation of their work and the impact of the factory project on the three villages involved. This participatory process of evaluation was used to ensure that the workers and many of the villagers were involved in the development of the project. The evaluation was commissioned by CUSO to help the workers understand the development of the project. I was hired to implement the evaluation and to document its process and results.

The evaluation included an extensive interview with each worker about their work, the functioning of the project, and their relationships with the villagers. Many of these interviews took place in the weavers' homes. Structured interviews with about 30 villagers and local authorities were carried out to gather background information for the evaluation and to assess community views of the project.

The findings of these interviews were translated into English, tabulated, and brought back to the workers in a series of evaluation meetings. The workers were able to assess the feedback from the interviews and determine what could be done to remedy some of the deficiencies or problems exposed. For example, the workers felt that something had to be done to support the villagers in Modipane and Matebele because of the feelings expressed in the interviews that the project was mainly for people from Oodi.

A major report, *Tapestry, Report from Oodi Weavers*, was published by the National Institute for Research in Development and African Studies, University College of Botswana, in 1977 and then reprinted in 1981. A 300-page dramatic record was produced. It is an account of how this small venture significantly altered the lives of the people and the physical development in three African villages. Only a third of the book that emerged from this effort was formal evaluation material. The main substance of the book documented the personal views of 12 village people, in their words, of what the project meant to them. The report wove a colourful story of a village and people in the throes of turbulent social and personal change, with its bright and dark spots, dynamism, and resistance. As part of the evaluation, the views of the manager at the time, Peder Gowenius, were also recorded, and these appear later in this chapter.

The Cooperative Members

A crucial aspect of sustaining production at the time (July 1977) appeared to be how well the workers had been included in meaningful decision making within the factory and, therefore, their management proficiency. If the worker body was able to manage the factory and continue production for at least a few years, it was felt that the long-range development objectives could possibly be accomplished. Thus, for two days the workers discussed (first in small groups, then together) major issues that affected them, the factory, and the villages. Based on these talks, they made decisions and instigated actions that would help improve their capacity to manage the factory. The discussions focused on issues that were considered concrete obstacles to the continued operation of the project, and the excerpts bring to light some of the specific day-to-day workings of the factory.

The following excerpts are taken directly from *Tapestry, Report from Oodi Weavers* (Lewycky 1977 and 1981, 197–204).

* * *

Who Are the Real Owners?

About ten per cent of the workers stated flatly they did not know who was the owner of the factory, while another 22 per cent wrongly stated that Peder and Ulla were the owners (after numerous "lectures" by

Peder, this probably indicates caution rather than ignorance). Of the remainder who said the workers owned the factory, many expressed doubts as to the validity of this ownership or what in fact it meant to be the owners of the factory. Therefore, the first issue discussed was this aspect of worker ownership of the factory.

Most of the workers said they did not understand the ownership or appreciate its importance because they had no concrete evidence that the factory was theirs. They said they had neither "paid out any money from our pockets" nor helped construct the factory buildings and therefore had no evidence that the factory belonged to them. They also noted that the project idea had come from outside their village and by Rra Masiza. Therefore, they had not been fully involved in the project from the beginning and could not be sure what had taken place to start it.

Other workers said they could understand the ownership of the factory for they had already paid for it through the labour "of our hands," but they expressed reservations and said they would believe they were the owners only when the Goweniuses were gone.

Therefore, the workers decided it was necessary to further discuss the history of the factory and that each worker would buy a membership card as evidence of ownership of the factory, similar to that received for participation in the local cooperative society.

What Is a Fair Wage?

Over half of the workers expressed dissatisfaction with their wages, not only the amount, but with the means by which wages were determined. They largely agreed that all were working equally towards the same factory goals and, therefore, all should be paid equally. They said they put in the same amount of time and, therefore, there was no difference in their work. As well, there was a prevailing concern over the uncertainty of how much they would receive each month.

Criticism of judging tapestries and bedspreads for determining bonuses was implicit in the wage discussion. The workers said this was responsible for much of the friction between workers and, therefore, should be removed. They thought the quality of production was generally high already and that individual desire to "make beautiful things" was sufficient incentive to continue high quality production without judging.

The decision was then to place all workers on a daily wage rate of P3 as of the next month. This was done after Peder reiterated his reasons for setting up the wage system as it had been and after he challenged the workers on what they would do if an individual's production dropped now that their wages were not dependent on their production level. The workers felt group pressure could be brought to encourage recalcitrant workers but that this would not likely be necessary, because they knew their jobs and what had to be done.

The judging would continue, but not to determine wages. Instead judging would continue to record the quality of individual weaves so they had the comparisons on which to evaluate their work. If there was a noticeable drop in quality, it was decided that some form of sanctions would be established.

What Will Happen When the Goweniuses Leave?

Recurring regularly in interviews with the workers was the fear of what would happen to the factory when the Goweniuses left. Over half of the workers expressed fears that there would be either fighting between workers or absolute confusion. Only 26 per cent said there would be no change in the operation of the factory, and one woman flippantly thought things would improve.

Part of the fear they expressed was due to a lack of confidence in themselves, as many of the workers said they did not have the general capacity to operate "such a large industry." There was also a lack of trust among the workers and an apparent resistance to cooperate, which the workers noted as reasons for their concerns. A third explanation for the fear was that they lacked management skills to run the factory.

It was agreed that a large part of the concern could only be alleviated by the workers' personal efforts to cooperate and get along in the factory. This, they implied, might improve now that the wages had been equalized and that the tapestry judging, the main source of conflict, had been altered. However, they also agreed with Peder that clearly stated rules or regulations for behaviour were required. Documented rules plus defined punishments for infractions would prevent one person taking responsibility for disciplining a fellow worker and this, therefore, would alleviate potential conflict.

Is the Management Committee Managing?

The fourth issue discussed concerned the function of the management committee. Clearly, many of the workers did not understand the reason for the MC or what the MC did on a daily basis. Just over half of the workers said the MC was there to manage the factory, but most of these expressed doubt as to what the management actually consisted of.

There was also a repeated call for the delegation of one manager for the factory. The workers said either someone should be appointed from outside the village, possibly from the government, or Mogapi, the assistant manager, should be delegated and trained as the manager. As one woman said, "Every child has a father." This concern ran contrary to Peder's design and management intent of the factory, and he, therefore, repeated his understanding of the flaws inherent in an elitist management system. "You call for a manager, for a leader," he said, "but you know that if you have one person over you, you will constantly try to bring him down. You would always try to rebel against his leadership."

As a compromise, the workers agreed to learn more about the MC and how it functioned and give it a chance to become operational. As a concrete measure, they agreed that the next MC meeting would be held before the entire worker body to show the operation of the committee and, therefore, inform others of its responsibilities.

Are the Villages Changing?

Because village development is an intrinsic part of the project, and the factory depends on the village for support, the workers also discussed a few issues pertaining to the local villages. First, Matebele and Modipane were discussed separately. The workers focused on two main questions: why was there less apparent development in these villages, and what could be done to help them develop?

The villagers of Matebele were most concerned about the unequal development of Oodi over Matebele. They felt severely handicapped by Oodi's size and legal dominance. They strongly stated the need for their own identity as a community and how being tied to Oodi was destroying their village. Some of the Matebele residents agreed the developments in Oodi were accessible to them (for example, the Consumers Cooperative), but maintained the need to bring some concrete improvements to their village to preserve its existence.

The factory workers agreed with the predominating Oodi attitude that Matebele was technically a part of Oodi and any development coming to the latter was equally for the former. They noted Matebele was smaller than Oodi originally and, therefore, could not expect to have equal improvements and services. However they did not totally reject the Matebele concerns, for they agreed that "those who sit on the outside of the fire can get cold," i.e., they were not receiving all the possible benefits they needed and deserved.

As a solution, the workers said the Matebele people should make more of an effort to come to Oodi to state their case and seek development possibilities for their village. The workers, therefore, missed the point of Matebele's concerns; however, they suggested a small industry of some sort for Matebele. Peder then said a small sewing unit (employing about ten women) was being planned but that there was a delay in securing the expatriate instructor.

The workers also proposed that a bridge be built between the villages to help the Matebele people cross to Oodi. Peder suggested seeking the assistance of the Roads Department, which was constructing a road through Oodi at the time. This was agreed unanimously but the workers noted that any assistance the factory offered should be done in conjunction with the people of Matebele via the headman and/or the Village Development Committee. It was then resolved that the assistant manager would discuss this idea with the village (a meeting took place three days later) and write to the Roads Department on behalf of the factory to build a bridge and grade a road.

For Modipane the situation was quite different. First the people of Modipane were less represented in the factory and were more resistant to cooperating with the factory. None of those interviewed from Modipane explained why there were so few from Modipane working and they did not acknowledge that most of those who had been working had quit without reason. However, the greatest problem they cited was the lack of local employment. Some of the local officials also noted they were ill informed about various activities in the factory which they thought they should know about.

The workers were obviously less kind to the Modipane people for they were accused of being too proud and unwilling to cooperate with Oodi people. Again the workers said these villagers should come to Oodi to discuss development issues if the former wanted to develop themselves, and that Modipane had a number of developments already and, therefore, did not have that much to complain about (e.g., health post, water, and a new road).

The workers reported reasons preventing worker assistance to Modipane. An internal conflict between the different village groups that make up Modipane, they said, was partially contributing to the lack of development within the village. An animosity that has existed between Oodi and Modipane for some time was also noted to explain why so few people from Modipane responded positively when the factory was started. The workers said the Modipane people had not trusted the idea of a factory and yet had wanted to have any new developments go to Modipane. These villagers were, therefore, less willing to participate in discussions with factory workers or people from Oodi.

However, the workers were initially split on what should be done. Some said that the factory should just wait until the people of Modipane came forward. They said nothing could be done until the people showed an interest in doing something for themselves. Others maintained that because Modipane people did not understand the factory, an effort should be made to help them. It was decided that the assistant manager would investigate the possibility of holding another tapestry exhibit in Modipane to inform the people about the factory. Two weeks later, accompanied by a videotape recording of the factory, the workers went to each of the project villages to promote the project.

Is There Cooperation in the Village?

One of the nebulous findings of the village survey was that there was a reluctance among villagers to work with other villagers. [This will be dealt with in greater detail in the next chapter.] Generally, people expressed the concern that the only way people would assist each other was if they were paid for their work. This lack of cooperation was expressed at different levels, from getting others to help in the lands to the lack of interest in *kgotla* meetings.

The workers agreed with this appraisal but clearly found it more difficult to discuss than the concrete issues covered earlier. However, they said the decreased cooperation was due to a lack of trust among villagers and fear of being cheated. Some said this was because of people actually being cheated; e.g., individuals trying to dominate syndicates or group businesses.

They said people would work together in the past only because of the Regiment system and the power of the Chief. Now, they said, people feel they can only benefit from their efforts if they receive money, i.e., individual benefits as opposed to group benefits.

Suggested solutions of this situation included, "more people should borrow from Sethunya," "people must stand up for themselves if they want something," and that there should be more jobs, for once people are earning money the workers felt they would cooperate more freely. No actions were offered to meet these suggestions.

Peder spoke to the workers (he called it "preaching") and said that the main intent of the factory project was to cultivate the cooperative spirit that appeared to be lacking in Botswana. He said that by working together in the factory, the workers could reject the contemporary trend towards self-interest and social fragmentation and, therefore, contribute to meaningful social development. He thought the continued existence of the factory, managed by the workers alone, would set a good example for, and make its greatest contribution to, the rest of the nation.

Does Anyone in the Village Notice?

Another general impression gleaned from talking with the villagers was that there was little understanding of what the factory could and did do for the village. Few acknowledged that the factory had any benefit for them, though they said the water and Cooperative shop (Consumers Cooperative) were definite improvements to the village and for themselves. Also some who said they did not benefit personally were closely related to workers and were receiving money from them. None noted the money the factory gave to the Burial Society or the Football Club and few mentioned the Sethunya loans. Of those who knew about the latter, only a small number said they understood how to get loans and showed they were well informed about the loans.

This issue seemed equally difficult for the workers to discuss as the question of cooperation. However, they said some of the reasons for the lack of understanding were similar to those affecting village cooperation, i.e., distrust, poor attendance at *kgotla*, and, therefore, misinformation. They also admitted that part of the reason was their lack of understanding of things such as Sethunya (on the questionnaire 32 per cent of the workers said they did not know what Sethunya was intended for).

A better informed public would result from more information taken to the villages, the workers decided. They suggested that the Sethunya Board of Trustees take a more active role in publicizing the loan service and that VDC's should be invited to discuss factory services with the MC. They also recommended that tapestry exhibits should be taken to the three villages again, for many people were at the lands in March and, therefore, more people could come this time. However, they noted that there must be a better understanding imparted to the workers first. This would have to be done by Rra Masiza continuing his lectures to the workers.

The Managers' Assessment

Peder and Ulla Gowenius first came to Southern Africa from Sweden in 1961. Dynamic, creative, and straightforward people, they started the Rorke's Drift Arts and Crafts Centre in South Africa and the Thabana Li méle Centre in Lesotho before coming to Botswana. Their two sons were born in Africa. They continue to create and teach art while farming in Sweden.

Above: The Cooperative compound — the showroom is on the left and the main work area is on the right.

Left: In April 1997, the management committee of the Cooperative met with Headman Molebatsi Semele and other important village members.

Below: Author Dennis Lewycky between weaver Tsietsi Mogapi and translator Shaka Mochine.

"From the Book of Tswana Tales," Mabifi Moeng and Dipou Matlapeng
145 X 209 cm

The story involves a girl with scars painted on her face. From the bottom to the top, she presents a drink to the chief, then turns into an anthill, from which she emerges free of scars.

Above: Oshale Tobane at her floor loom, weaving a blanket.

Left: In the spinning room, wool is prepared for weaving.

Below: The weavers often weave traditional Batswana designs or symbols into high-quality woolen blankets.

Above: "At the Clinic,"
Batshedi Mothoosele and
Monyana Moloi
102 X 145 cm
The family welfare
educator works at the
village clinic (the white
building).

Right: Weaver Dora
Tlhagwane working on a
wild-animal scene.

Above: "The Traditional Wedding," Lebogang Sekolo
140 X 120 cm

Below: "Ploughing Season," Mosire Morake
148 X 138 cm

Above: In 1977, Grace Balole wove the historical "Bewitching the Factory" tapestry with Dipugo Masilo.

Right: Grace (Balole) Ncube is now a successful farmer and business-woman in Matebele.

Above: Itshekeng Molwantwa was a spinner in the project in 1977.

Left: She is now a tapestry weaver and chair of the management committee. She often represents the cooperative at public events.

Left: Diana Meswele was farming near Oodi when first interviewed 20 years ago. She is now a member of the Village Development Committee, and is shown here addressing National Service participants in 1997.

Below: "Untitled," Tidimalo Tlhagwane 146 X 118 cm
This tapestry depicts two women's groups — the burial society and members of the YWCA.

Above: The opening of Lentswe la Oodi Weavers brought villagers and national dignitaries together (1974).

Left: Ulla Gowenius provided most of the weaving instruction (1977).

Below: Peder and Ulla Gowenius take advantage of the winter sun (1977).

Above: Manager of the Cooperative, Josephina Mogadi, at her desk (1997).

Right: Kgomotso Tlhagwane greets visitors in the Cooperative's showroom (1997).

Below: Blankets and runners are woven on floor looms — tapestries are woven on vertical looms (right).

To a large degree it is their passionate commitment to social ideals that gave birth to and established the character of the Oodi Weavers project. To complete a description of the project and its history, it is, therefore, important to understand their perspectives on the project and the human dynamics that they saw as part of the process of social change taking place in Botswana in the 1970s.

The following is a composite interview that came out of numerous discussions between Peder and myself in 1977. For convenience and in this case only, Ulla let Peder speak for both of them. In 1997, Peder and Ulla then reviewed this section of the book, without making any changes to the text. Peder also plans to write his own assessment of the weavers' experience in the near future.

Peder Gowenius

Artistic Influences

More or less everyone who comes to the factory asks three main questions, that is, if they even bother to ask questions. "Who makes the designs?" is the most common question, and then, "Where do the raw materials come from?" There is an underlying comment that if it is imported then the project is a failure or at least useless. The third question is about counterpart training.

Now if you start with the question of design, it is the mistrust where people do not believe that the weavers can make the designs themselves. We constantly have people asking, "Do these people r-e-a-l-l-y design their own weaves?" They mean, of course, "Do these Black people really design the weaves?" for they just can't believe it. I sometimes think they are pretty insulting.

There is some of our influence in the designs — there is no doubt about that — but the influence was in the first two years when I went around the weaves and said, "This is excellent," or "This is perfect," or "I like this a lot." Encouragement. But very rarely did anyone have to completely change what they had done. And then there is an influence at the end of the month when we judge. But with the stories, well I often tell the story, or give the idea, but they will translate it into a weave . . . arrange the design. But most of the time the stories come from something that happened in the workshop, in the village, or in the country. I might make a very rough sketch, but this is for maybe one in ten weaves. But to come and say that I make the designs or deny that the weavers make the designs is ridiculous and a clear sign of the so-called experts' complete lack of trust in the people, and often a sign of White superiority.

The reason they can express themselves and make these designs and, within a comparatively short time, produce articles that are sought after by museums and art galleries, is because they have never expressed themselves in this way before. They have taken a short cut. We all have barriers to overcome in producing art. If you teach art in Europe you'll see we have all the hang-ups about what is good or what is bad . . . all that we have been taught about art. So you have to retrain or re-educate, strip them of their restrictive knowledge and beliefs about what is art. But here you don't have to do that, for the weaver quickly learns the technique, then after a while there comes a time in every weaver's development where she starts to become critical of herself or her work. Some don't develop further but a few do become what I call true artists, that is, going from being a weaver to being an artist. I think among the weavers there are two who have shown they are artists and a few more who might yet develop. So we have three or four, of about 20 tapestry weavers, and that is about the proportion anywhere of people who have the desire to express themselves and the imagination required.

Expressing a Culture

There is also the related question: "Is this traditional African art?" And when you answer flatly, "NO," — because you get tired of this question — they just say, "Ah . . . it's just the Scandinavian influence then." But you have to remember that all people carry a tradition, carry a culture of their own, and there are no people without this tradition. Sometimes this culture has expressed itself in dancing, music, or words, and sometimes pictures. Now in Botswana one can generally say that it has expressed itself in words, in language, and in song partially. But it has never come out visually. If you give people the medium to express this tradition, you will only help express that culture more. You carry out a tradition in a way that it has never been put before, but it still comes from the people, so it is a part of their culture. Using a new medium is part of their historical development in expressing their culture. I mean it takes time to break away from the influence of the teacher and the medium to go further, but this comes with confidence, if you believe in what you are doing and enjoy it.

At the initial stage in the factory you could see that it was only money the weavers wanted, and then there was a gradual growth of joy in their work, as such, in the weaves and in the stories. There was a gradual understanding of weaving as a medium and with that understanding they started to slowly connect the weaving to their traditions.

So if you ask if this is traditional, you can say yes or no bluntly, because that is an easier way of getting out of such a narrow question. But in Botswana, it is the first time the tradition has expressed itself visually, except for what the Basarwa have done on a limited scale. I just really get tired of experts saying this is not really African or that these colours are typically African . . . they are just revealing their western textbook understanding of art.

Now you may ask if the quality of the weaves will go down when Ulla and I leave. Well, when we went on leave for three months, the quality did go down because the confidence and the connection between their tradition or culture and the medium wasn't firmly established. It was still in a floating situation. I think the chances are better now, but if the weavers start to weave for requests and conform to commercial demands, they will fail to broaden their artistic abilities. The tapestries do not have sufficient roots in the society to continue alone yet. So we have to, in some way, make the weavers struggle with their art so they do not just weave tapestries technically but put themselves into their weaves. We make them struggle or challenge their skills through the stories they weave. I give them sufficiently complicated stories and deliberately choose subjects to develop their apparent abilities. If you take Mmanaughty, for example, she has been doing faces and I want her to move from the faces to the hands, so I have put people in chains this time so she can practise on hands. She is now bored with faces, and doing something new, like the hands, will make her struggle again.

You must remember that the factory and the production process are there primarily to establish confidence and awareness. The art side and the cultural side support this very definitely. For example, if you were to make mouse traps in this kind of factory your chances would be considerably less that you could build confidence. Here you can create something you and others can appreciate and, therefore, it is not just the production process which you learn from, but a combination of culture, tradition, and the production process.

A Raw Issue of Raw Materials

Now let's look at this question of where the raw materials come from and, of course, to whom you sell these things. But you know, here you have the liberals or textbook socialists who believe the raw materials must come from inside the country, otherwise whatever you do is useless. They want to develop within the resources of the country. They say we should not produce luxury articles for export or for sale to expatriates, but that you should produce mouse traps, burners, and pots that can be used by the people. Now these things are needed and important, but the talk is clear, forward, bloody stupidity, because it is based on a complete lack of understanding of economic realities. These people asking the question have gone to a certain degree of awareness, but do not understand the economic realities of Botswana. South Africa is the extremely dominant financial centre of Southern Africa, and we are on the periphery of it. We are pressed down so much by this dominance that to think we can challenge that in a small way by producing small things for a local market is ridiculous. What we can produce for a local market is so limited; the result is that the producer, the worker, gets almost nothing. At this stage it is important to produce things so that the workers get as much as possible out of their efforts . . . so that she or he does not feel forced to go to the Republic to work. You then back up a feeling of nationhood, of self-reliance, and of independence.

Consider the psychological implications if you produce paraffin lamps, which are needed here; but in its own way it looks inferior to the one from the Republic of South Africa (RSA) — it looks bad, not as polished. And because of the capital costs and the machinery needed, and to price it to be a little more competitive to RSA, the workers get very little money. So when you try to sell the lamp, no one wants to buy it because it is almost the same price but it doesn't look as smart. The result is that people start to feel inferior. The guy making the lamp starts to feel, "Is this all that I can do? While on that side of the border we can make something so much nicer and better." So you don't get a feeling of pride or nationhood. If you examine just what can be produced here that is competitive to a highly industrialized society, there is almost nothing. So we can make [concrete blocks for building construction]. Can we make cement? No! Why can't we make cement? Because we need certain raw materials. Are these materials here? Then you could not produce enough to be competitive. And so on.

Now if the border was closed, if we were completely cut off from South Africa, then you must talk about the raw materials, then you must talk about the local markets. But while the border is open it's ridiculous to talk about it. Close the border and we will change our production to a local market and we will use local raw materials. But then we will have to mechanize, or at least semi-mechanization will come. We will be forced to move from hand weaving to machines and this will mean fewer employees. And wages will go down to keep the costs down, but at least we would no longer have to compete for the market.

Counterpart Training

The other question I'm asked concerns a manager: "Are we training someone to replace us?" Well, project after project after project has failed to do this — that is, train a counterpart — and I think this approach is wrong right from the start because it is psychologically wrong. First, a Motswana doesn't have that much job opportunity and, therefore, he goes for the money rather than his interests or even his abilities. He doesn't even know if he will like the work before he starts to be trained as the counterpart. So he and the expatriate are put into a rigid situation where the expert is expected to teach the Motswana, and both will react negatively to being forced into this situation. Especially in Botswana where there are still feelings of inferiority among the Blacks, the Motswana will eventually rebel against this forced situation. And there are the cultural differences that prevent good communication. The expert with his knowledge built on technological information will dominate the counterpart, who gains his knowledge largely from human experience. They think differently. And if the expatriate does not listen to his counterpart, he will make mistakes and he will be considered a fool. Before long they are not going to be getting along.

Then you are given one or two years to train this person to do your job. The time factor will push you, and it does not come natural. Somebody else likely selected the counterpart for you, and you may not get along because you have different personalities. But the correct procedure in the factory is that everyone is trained in the production process for two years, then you select 12 or 13 workers and, from these, you select one who could be the manager. Possibly this could work.

The fact that we don't want a traditional type of manager in the factory is another reason against a counterpart. First, there is a tendency in this society to challenge everyone immediately; that is, there is constant small politicking going on — jealousies. I feel that if you put one guy in charge, and if he is one of your own, everybody will say, "Let's knock him down, kill him." At the same time, there is always this call for leadership. The whole political situation in Southern Africa is suffering because of this call for leadership. So people who try to take the lead are brought down. My theory — which is greatly simplified because we cannot deal properly with all the things we should in the time we have — is that people have been under the South Africa "boss" system for so long, with the White boss protected by the police and the law and the whole apartheid system backing him up, that the Black man reacts violently against other Black men when he is given the chance. If he challenges the Whites, he is knocked down and locked up, or if he is too straightforward he is killed. So when there is a Black boss, they think "Here is my chance to knock him down." And this is not necessarily deliberately from awareness, but it is a subconscious release of something from within. It is a reflex action. Later they may realize that this man was helping them.

Another aspect is that people in Southern Africa also have this fear, all the time, that in some way they are being cheated. If you have one man in charge the blame will be put on him. At present the blame is with me, and they don't challenge it because I am White. But when I leave, the blame will be on Mogapi [the assistant manager at the time] and they will challenge him.

I mean it is obvious that the people are being cheated. For example, in Lesotho the people took their wool to the local store and it was weighed on the scale and then the seller got a paper that stated how much he could receive in goods for the value of the wool. Now everybody felt cheated — if they knew the scale and if they could calculate the prices themselves, they would not be so suspicious. They could be sure they got the correct price. And, of course, some were cheated. So that is why I believe as many workers as possible should know how to do different things in the factory.

We have gone over the calculation of wages with the workers a number of times, and still after all these years, some people still claim they do not understand it. Partially they say this because they are afraid you'll ask them to explain in detail and they don't want to answer or be put on the spot. But still I'm certain that many still feel cheated. They may go to a friend and get help to calculate their wages and then they are satisfied they are not cheated. On a few occasions, they come to the office and say something was forgotten, and in every case they have been right, which means they know what their wage is and how it is determined, how to work it out. Now if this wage procedure was not explained to them, then every wage day they would go home and be unsatisfied . . . feel cheated.

And this is tied to years of exploitation, for they *have* been cheated. If you agree to pay a man P12 a month, you have not cheated him, for you have made an agreement; but he will feel cheated, for he thinks he should be paid more. He sees you sitting in a big house and driving a car, and he sees himself unable to feed himself, so he is cheated. He is not cheated, for you had an agreement with him for the wages, but he is cheated because of the inequalities of the society.

There are so many things wrong with the idea of one manager, such as the social traditions. If you are a young man and you are related to somebody in the factory, then you cannot tell him anything. Also, your "uncle" will expect favours from you because he is your senior. Then if you say, "Well, then bring in an outsider, like from Mochudi or Kanye," that person will be rejected and treated as an outsider . . . he just hasn't anything to say in this village. You can see that with the teachers and community workers.

The temptations for the manager to run away with the money are great. The pressures to swindle money are great in a society like this, and I can understand it. He is cornered by all these other social pressures working against him and he then says, "Why should I be working for you people?" He becomes desperate and will swindle or neglect his work. This doesn't always happen, but by far it is too dangerous.

What's the Answer for Management?

This would seem to lead towards expatriate managers, but if you do want to localize and put Batswana in these positions, you cannot rely on expatriates. It is true that expatriates do have a privileged position — you don't have roots in that society, for you just come and go. But to localize, then I say you can only turn to a management committee like we have here. We have a group of the workers, staying in the production process, but responsible for the management as representatives of the rest of the workers.

If, for example, I stay here and run this factory until I die, it will continue if I am not challenged from the top or the bottom. People would have work, they would get a wage and, of course, I would not be satisfied with the P250 a month I get now. But there would not be any of what we refer to as development, except the employment factor. If that is all the country wants, then maybe I should stay on. Incidentally, if I did want to keep this factory profitable I would keep the exact same management system, for I think it is the most economic. But you can then forget about things like confidence, self-reliance, and independence.

Perhaps the time is not ready for these things, I just don't know. I do know that if I stayed, the workers would not set down roots. The people will come and go, and they would not be seriously interested in the work other than in the money they get. They would not be part of the work. They would turn their money into drunkenness and they would not be interested in changing their village or helping others to improve.

But if you are concerned about changing this country, developing it, then things like the management committee, decentralization of decision making, and a broad educational programme are required. The way we do things in the factory is not only because of ideology, but because it is the only practical way, the only way of getting things done, and the only way of really helping this country.

Pedagogy

But remember I'm just throwing out statements that I'm not backing up, but hopefully someone will challenge what I say and in this way the dialogue which is so necessary will continue. Sometimes I'm in a position where I have to hit someone in the face with a statement so they will get mad, be challenged enough to react in some way. And I do this in the factory. I challenge the workers and even unfairly at times. I even insult them sometimes but then I do the opposite. But I think it is a matter of keeping the dialogue alive, that there is a dialogue. With an insult you may kill the dialogue but you may give a boost to something in the person. When I insult I think the dialogue has died away but I do not do this deliberately, that is, sit back and consider what is the best action. I take the situation as it comes and if I see something that is positive, that is good, I speak out.

This can be dangerous, of course, but it would be catastrophic if intentional. So if I insult someone I will not say it again for a few days or a week, because I have said it, I have made the point. And I think I am also prepared to be insulted, for I have been insulted, quite a few times. I don't take it as an insult, for when we know each other fairly well, you get over your fear of communicating and you are not on your alert all the time. You react to others just like you react to your wife or children or your relatives.

And, of course, I constantly make mistakes in this way. But if I didn't make mistakes I wouldn't be human, I wouldn't be a good teacher. To be a teacher you must make mistakes. I mean that in the relationship between teacher and student, there must be dialogue. This dialogue can only happen if there are signs of mutual respect. Now my respect towards the workers is built on years of experience in Southern Africa, where I again and again have seen people who have learnt to express themselves in a beautiful way. It is quite fantastic what a person with very little formal schooling can pick up in a very short time, once he or she is seriously interested and has the confidence required. Confidence and knowledge are dependent on one another. Sometimes the way the workers challenge me also puts respect in me. Their respect for me is less in what I say than in what I do, like the things they can see out of my work. Because I am somehow too far removed — put up by society — I have to be human to come down from that position.

Making Collective Decisions

Then the workers, I think, make mistakes also, and that is the way it should be. Last year, some of the women were interested in starting a nursery, a crèche for their children and other women in the village. They organized themselves and I think what they wanted to do was a good idea. When they brought it to the whole group of workers, the idea was defeated. The workers said they wanted to receive their year-end bonus rather than pay it into this crèche. I think this was wrong, they should have contributed to something for the village instead of taking for themselves only. But I could not say anything. It was their decision. In fact, it was much later that I found that they gave themselves their bonuses because they wanted some evidence that they could make decisions and I would not interfere. So they knew what was important to them at the time.

In the ordinary relationship between student and teacher, the teacher usually fails to understand that he or she is also a student. He thinks he must "teach" everything to this group or, in the case of counterpart training, to this guy who is taking over, and he does this from a superior position. So he sits on a fairly high chair and tries to teach someone sitting at his knees. And the man at his knees is constantly worrying whether he is doing his work right or if the master is satisfied with him. He is afraid to challenge him and yet he is fed up with the master's mistakes. The relationship as such does not allow the right communication for teaching, not the right framework for mutually beneficial communication.

And I know that most people are honestly trying to teach, but apparently they don't. Very seldom do we see it working. The expert leaves and the counterpart takes over and he gets in a mess and is fed up. We have seen this happen again and again. There are exceptions, but why don't people start to realize that something is wrong? The teacher is usually not humble enough to learn, and the student has a lot to teach about how his people react and think in a country like this. The student can say this is not acceptable or this approach will work. But the expert will come from a different culture and will push through his ideas instead of communicating. The student will see things going wrong, uncertain about himself and unable to challenge the teacher, usually because of a lack of technical ability or language, and he will withdraw from the teaching situation. I make exactly the same mistakes here.

If anyone at this place has been unfairly treated, it has been the assistant manager, Mogapi. I have this tendency not to consult, to talk things over, I just go ahead. I talk things over with the workers more than with Mogapi, for I always take it for granted that he has understood or he already knows something. This is part of the psychological barrier in the counterpart system. I think Mogapi has been confused about his position and I would say our relation is a fairly typical one, for I'm comparatively sensitive and I know about the dangers and still I've been unable to manage it. So in the factory, by keeping an educational dialogue going, we try to avoid the counter-productive teacher-student problem, at least to some degree. We try to create a dialogue where the workers learn what they think is important and at their pace.

Ready to Learn

This timing of learning is important. For example, we could not start the management training until the workers themselves were ready to learn. In any situation, your success in teaching always depends on the requirement that the student wants what you are teaching and knows why he wants the knowledge. When the student sees this, then you can start teaching. If you start too early, there will be a poor response, and by the time they can appreciate what you are teaching, they are becoming bored. The timing is crucial.

The timing is important in another way when you consider the process of learning, for in some ways we are creating a small elite here — assisting a small group of individuals rather than the community we claim. But it is a matter of backing up the individual first, before trying to stimulate the cooperative spirit, the community spirit. It is a matter of teaching the individual his capabilities and giving him the confidence to break out of the restricted system he is in. And you must provide for their physical needs. It is a matter of praxis, of more than just talking about such things as the relationship between one's effort and productivity.

Therefore, we designed the wage system so that each weaver felt the need for individual effort, and this is tied to their wages. I think they have seen this, and the equal wage they have decided upon will be better, but it could not have been this way if they had not learnt the basic relationship first. But because we saw the need to pay competitive wages to the wages in South Africa, we created a class of people much better off than the great majority in the village.

In order to avoid the creation of a class structure, in order to keep the workers part of the village, a levelling-out effect was required. That is partially why we started the Sethunya development fund for the villagers, so that the workers remain part of their villages and their village structure and contribute to it. It was also a question of their awareness, so they could contribute to the development of others, to the village, and to the country, a social awareness in order to balance the negative effects of backing up the individual, at an earlier stage. And then of course why the hell should they be better off? They should contribute to the village, but they could not appreciate this until they understood and had some control over their own situation.

And in this teaching I don't think you try to be liked or popular. I don't think you can be. You can see that I am comparatively withdrawn here. I am not very much in the village. To some extent I concentrate entirely on the work, because we are trying to create independence through confidence, but realistically we have made a lot of people comparatively dependent on us. But you have to fight this — to be aware of this all the time. I fight it by not going into the village too much, or sometimes by being rude or sometimes functioning like a boss. I sacked quite a number of people in the first two years, knowing quite well that I was functioning like a boss. And I put up high demands on productivity and expect workers to arrive on time. I don't lend money to people, and these are just some of the little ways we try to counter the dependence and support independence.

There is also a danger of becoming too removed from the village, from the people, but you have to walk a dangerous line. And you can fall on either side, and you sometimes do fall, and then become like a clown on the line; people must laugh at your ridiculous behaviour. But you must stumble and catch the line at the last moment and pull yourself up and keep going.

When We Leave

Okay, let's get back to this question of the counterpart. It is largely because of this counterpart idea that when the project starts to fail, as we have seen time and time again, another expatriate is brought in to save it. The counterpart is not trained sufficiently, he becomes disappointed, and eventually the project starts to slide down. Bringing in the new expatriate will not succeed in saving the project. He will try to bring in his own ways of doing things, his new ideas. Or if he is sensitive and understands the situation, he will try to fit into what is already existing; but either way he will fail because he will be confronted by the expectations of how things were done before. He may not try to change the project, but by the mere fact that he is new, he will be considered to be against the status quo; he will appear to be disruptive. He will fail, for the people will blame him for anything that goes wrong and he will blame the people. This confrontation will never allow the project to build itself up again to what it was.

Worker Confidence

So what is the solution? Well, I've already said enough about the management committee and the need to make the workers part of the management process of their own factory. But I firmly believe that when we come here to start a project like this, there must be a long-term commitment; so that we say we will remain until we have done all that we can, there is nothing more we can do, and the people have a good chance to take it over, continue the project without us. No other expatriate should have to move in behind you. So when we came here we said we would stay four to six years, and we will leave after four and a half. Possibly we could stay on a little longer or even leave earlier, but when we leave I think we would have given them as fair a chance as we can to run this factory on their own. We have given them the technical knowledge and they have the skills, but it is also a matter of confidence. In fact, the technical training is to back up the confidence so they can feel they are able to run the factory, able to maintain production.

At this stage, I don't think they have the knowledge, and there is the question remaining of whether they have the confidence. In the sales, for example, there are four women who are able to sell, but when expatriate customers come in, the women are not yet able to give the customer that extra push to make a sale. But this training has just started and I think they will have the skills before long. But it is still the matter of confidence — for if they believe they can manage the place, then they can manage the place. So are they at that stage? Well, no, they are not at that stage, but if we do not leave now, they will never arrive at that stage. We must go now to give them the chance. But I believe that the knowledge, the skills, and the experience they have now are enough to give some security to continue on their own. The confidence will develop. It is similar to teaching someone to ride a horse. You can teach the technique, then lead the horse from in front and then from behind, but the student will be afraid the first time alone. Once she/he knows they can do it, then they will have the confidence. You have to stay with the teaching long enough, so that the student has enough skills and enough confidence to try, and though they will be afraid at first, they must do it.

Fears About the Project

It is just if an accident or something happens early on to challenge the students, that there is a danger. And this is where I have my fears about the project, that outside forces will interfere with the factory before the workers have the confidence to deal with these new situations or problems. It is as if a dog runs in front of the horse and the student falls off before being sufficiently skilled. This is where the weakness of the project is. We are trying something in this society which is too far ahead for it, too advanced for its development. We are trying things like worker ownership and control, which will come in ten or twenty years, I'm sure, but now we are so isolated that very few people understand what we are doing.

This lack of understanding may allow outside forces to move against the project and destroy aspects of it, such as the self-reliance. Without knowing, and with good intentions, someone who does not understand the project may interfere. For example, we are trying to develop self-reliance, not only in the factory itself but in the minds of the workers. So when we built this bridge in the village, it was to move towards self-reliance by telling the villagers that independence is more than just slaughtering cattle and drinking beer, but that it is an opportunity to support the government by doing something for themselves. To show they could contribute something. And the bridge was built by the workers and the villagers, but the authorities in the council felt threatened in some way. They are struggling for power and this initiative in some way is challenging their power, their positions. You see this again and again in the country, where people do something for themselves and they are blocked and frustrated by bureaucracy, or authority, or even petty officials. In Matebele, the people built their own school but later the council tore it down and built another one. In Naledi, the people were making concerts and working towards their own schools and contributing to it until the Swedes built a beautiful nursery for them.

We try to build self-reliance but there are so many examples of actions working counter to it. In the case of the factory, there are so many forces that could use their little authority to change what we have been doing here and what has already been started. They will interfere, not necessarily because these people will want to destroy the place, but they will try to move into the factory, possibly to gain some form of power or just because they are concerned about the factory.

For instance, someone could say we will give you an accountant because we see you are weak in your bookkeeping. The accountant will not understand all the reasons for setting up the factory as it is and how it is being run, but will use his knowledge and influence to change the factory. Because the workers are not knowledgeable in that area and because they are intimidated by him, they will follow. But if we can give the workers one or two years to run the factory on their own, they will then have the confidence. If the problem arises at an early stage, then they are lost. But no outside body can help them at this stage, regardless of how well-intentioned or how understanding of the project, for the workers must do it alone for one or two years. Then if they decide they want outside help, it is different . . . they will see the needs and how to cope. Any aid moving in without this awareness will destroy the factory.

For example, Rorke's Drift is still going on and is considered a success, but at the time we left, I considered the project a failure. It was a success in terms of what some call development buildings, quality of art work, number of students and number of teachers — all the physical things. But it never had any roots in the society, and the reason it didn't was because at the time I didn't realize the development needs of the people. I thought training was enough and that by setting up a school the students could do the rest. We realized too late that there is a need for village involvement and control by the workers. It is the church or the mission that controls the place and dominates it. The people don't believe it is theirs because it is not theirs. There is no commitment from them, and it is slowly tapering off.

In Lesotho, on the other hand, we were almost carried away by what could be called a people's movement. There was an enormous interest in Thabana Li méle, where many applied, and there was a steady stream of visitors. Nothing like here. There were seven or eight groups a day at times, riding down from the most remote villages to see what we were doing, to ask questions. We were pushed by the people and we couldn't meet the demand for technical training or production units. But then it was closed down and we were kicked out, and about a year later a U.N. project reopened it. This did not work because the "expert" manager was incompetent and supposedly corrupt, and the project flopped. But I think generally it was more of a success than Rorke's Drift, because it gave the people a reference into the future. People will remember when there was hope for it, and they will remember what was good about it. The people still talk about it, way up in the mountains, the positive things in it were carried on. There it has had an impact, and educationally it has been a success. They saw hope in it.

Village Politics

Here I fear that petty village politics may destroy the factory. When the government changed the political system in the country, centralized it, they did not adequately explain the change to all the people. So now you have uninformed people and others playing the village authorities off the council authorities. Or individuals in their desire for power will make it difficult for others who they think opposed them. I can see the council in Mochudi destroy the project with their best intentions. These government officials or others from different aid agencies could destroy the factory by not understanding it and not understanding that any aid at this time would have only negative impact.

But if everyone leaves them alone for at least a year they will do a good job. I have faith that they will not fail and that is why I think we can leave. Of course there may be a drop in sales initially but only a small drop and possibly there will be a decline in the quality of the weaves. This may happen for a few years, but then it will come up again. We are establishing a reputation already and this I think will maintain the market. But the workers will gain confidence in their work and they will see the benefits in their work. And this confidence I can never give, for it will only come from the fact that they do manage themselves.

National Development

Part of my fear of interference is because of a feeling that we are too early in the development of this country. Much of what is happening in this country is contrary to what we are trying to teach. There is talk of self-reliance, independence, and nationhood, and we are trying to create these, but there is so little evidence of that in the country. The Brigades are trying, I suppose. There is the migrant labour system, on the other hand, which takes young men to the mines and which the country seems to be encouraging rather than stopping. So we have young men going to the mines instead of staying in Botswana and developing a sense of nationhood or a feeling for their country. They treat Botswana as a holiday resort, somewhere they come to drink and have fun. They are not developing their own confidence in themselves to move the country ahead.

When the men do come back to Botswana to work, we have to re-educate them. We have to somehow show them the negative effects of the "boss-boy" system, for in South Africa you work when the boss looks, and when the boss turns away, you stop working. If you didn't work that way, if you didn't function that way, you couldn't survive. But here this attitude is harmful to the country. In all fairness, this government is still not locked into one type of development. There are still open doors and the idea of democracy is still valid. There are many open doors, unlike in some countries, where people can keep trying different ways. The country is still open to all kinds of alternatives for development. The fact that we were allowed to start is evidence of this.

Where I think the government has failed is in politicizing the people, to give them a sense of nationhood, of unity or of strength. The President has stressed this need a number of times in his own speeches. But nothing has been done. You can say that the migrant labour does some good, it does bring in some money, but what many people neglect to consider is what could be done if the men stayed in Botswana. I think the psychological effects on things like self-reliance and a sense of nationhood are catastrophic.

But it is like standing in the desert and shouting, "This is a nation, we have to develop it." You are very much alone and you feel very much alone. You don't feel you get the support. Take this exhibition in Sweden now, at a very good museum, and we have requests from others. Several high officials get to know about the factory, but how many have ever been out here to see us? How many have shown an interest in what we are doing? And with things like the trade fair or the tenth anniversary celebrations, there were so many things we could do to display our tapestries but no one ever thinks of these things. We could have had a good exhibition at the Gaborone Museum at the time but instead we had to go to Mochudi to exhibit. At the trade fair we just get a corner.

All right, so people have read about Lentswe la Oodi but how many really know what it is? If we wrote out our objectives and goals on a placard, how many would read what it says? When we exhibit in Gaborone at the mall, very few stop to look, but if you went to Tanzania or Nigeria you would get a quite different response. There was this art festival in Nigeria this year (FESTAC '77), but no one considered that Lentswe la Oodi Weavers could represent Botswana; instead, they sent some "observers." And I'm certain we could have had a good impact on that festival, and Botswana would be advertised.

I just don't know why there seems to be so little interest in what we are doing here. I mean initially there were a few Batswana who worked for the district council who came here, but they were transferred and no others have come. Possibly a couple have come to see the factory, but I can count them on one hand. And yet we get lots of publicity, so people should know something about the factory; we even get lots of encouragement and official support from the government. I think it is only [Cabinet Minister] Dr. Chiepe who has come out here unofficially to see what we are doing, and [Cabinet Minister] Mr. Mogwe sent a very complimentary and encouraging telegram from Sweden when he saw our exhibit there, but there have not been any other people who have shown an interest. Can you explain this? There is no sense of nationhood, and the people just do not take an interest in what is happening in their country. I think it all ties into the lack of any national feeling. In Lesotho, we were just carried away by the public interest; even [Prime Minister] Chief Jonathan was out to the factory four times in the two years we were there. All the ministers were there, and the university frequently arranged tours of the centre.

The Market Place

One comment that visitors make about Botswana may give us the key to this situation. If they have travelled in other African countries, they always note that there are no market places here and nobody seems to be doing anything in the way of business. Why is that? Well, I think if we look into history we see that the people who came to Botswana were pushed here from other parts of Southern Africa by the White man and, therefore, all the people in Botswana were, at one time or another, refugees. Before they had recovered and built their own society here, the Whites were here after them . . . the missionaries and traders. The missionaries never gave them the chance to develop their nationhood, culturally.

The people were culturally oppressed right from the beginning. The traders never gave the people the chance to establish their own businesses or a sense of business. They have never recovered. The missionaries brought in their new thoughts and ideas. The traders brought money and goods and, therefore, immediately tied Botswana to South Africa. Even a small trader today cannot get started because of the large traders and the capital they control. So when the Botswana Development Corporation invites companies like Frasers and Metro [large South African department stores] to come in, they will monopolize the trade even further to the South African side.

It was different in Lesotho, because the Whites pushed the Basothos into the hills, but the hills belonged to them before anyway — it was still their home. In the 50 years of struggle, these people gained confidence and strength in themselves as a nation and largely because they were not smashed down by the Whites. They never lost a battle — it was starvation that finally defeated them.

The Struggle for Nationhood

We don't necessarily have to say that the Batswana, therefore, need a war to create nationhood, but what they need is the struggle. In my opinion, the government should stop the flow of migrant labour, for example, which might lose some money at first, but which would have very important psychological benefits. The struggle to survive would create this sense of nationhood. They need to struggle and not fall back on the South African economy or its cash.

In the way that the missionaries and traders dominated a weak society, in the same way I think the expatriates in this country are far too dominant. We never give the country a fair chance to develop its nationhood. But one can say that since independence a lot of things have happened, and it is true; but these are physical things — what is often called "development." But the understanding of these things among the majority of the people is nil. So one can say, therefore, that nothing has happened. But we have to accept that definition of development. I believe, though, that if the human being is not a part of development, and they have little understanding of it, you will at some stage get a strong counteraction.

If you don't involve people in the development of these physical benefits and services, then you ignore the most important part of development. Health and water are important but if you don't involve people you destroy their dignity and you create things like apathy, indifference, and complacency. Now nothing will go wrong as long as the crutches — the expatriate, for example — remain. But if we believe the country must truly be independent and we don't want an expatriate-supported system indefinitely, then superficial development is unacceptable. Let's not forget that the person is the most important resource and development factor, and that it should not be neglected because of the other economic factors. Take away a person's goals or whatever he needs to look forward to, and you create confusion — you force the person to cope with the situation in the best way he knows, and that is usually drinking.

Another effect of this expatriated form of development was that when these third world nations gained independence, they all called for education, but it was an education they did not understand. I think that all African leaders had the right intentions, but the experts and the technicians moved in and the educational system that resulted did not create self-confidence and was not relevant to the society. It resulted in dependencies rather than independence and self-reliance. But to bring people back into development still requires education — the question is, what kind of education?

Self-reliance

This I suppose comes down to the realization that this project is completely wrong. It is still trying to impose certain values and criteria on the Batswana, even if these try to develop confidence and self-reliance so that the people can create the type of society they want. It is well-intentioned but I think it is no better than some aspects of colonialism. You can't even use the most legitimate of arguments that we must do something rather than do nothing. We still perpetuate a system that is basically destructive. I don't know of any African country where the expatriates have such a high profile, and I think this definitely should be limited. And yet I think the technical skills we can provide are still important.

I sometimes think we have not progressed at all, for it is such a long-term process. It is a matter of making people aware of their potential and building their confidence so they can take hold of their lives for their own benefit. It takes a matter of decades to change the ingrained beliefs and fears. If there was more support from this country, if there were more actions directed in the same direction we are aiming at, then I could expect greater changes, for there would be better understanding. If teachers, district government staff, health personnel, and on and on were all geared in the same direction, then we could have come a lot further. In some ways it is amazing we have moved at all.

The workers have started to see the direction, but in the village I doubt if we have even indirectly affected their direction. Communication or dialogue has started where people have started to talk or think about the different aspects of development. For example, the people of Modipane have started to demand jobs, which shows they have started to see the value of their own efforts, while some people continue to say they want health clinics and water or bridges. There may be a little dialogue started.

I suppose it frightens me that so many expatriates come into this country and are not aware of the complexity of the situation. They are not aware of the basic economic constraints or the political needs of the people. These expatriates usually have no knowledge of the historical conditions that created this country as it is today. I hope that you now have a better understanding of the situation here and its complexity — a better understanding of what is meant by the word "development." But we still move into this country, disregard the people, and try to impose our own ways of living and our own values, which, incidentally, are also destroying our own countries. We cannot get to know the common person here, we cannot communicate adequately — granted — but we don't even make the effort to try to learn or hear what the people have to say.

Three Women Speak

In this book, it is not possible to include all the knowledge and experience the individual weavers have about their factory. However, it is useful to include some personal perspectives on the factory experience and work in general, as well as how the project functioned in the start-up years. The following are three accounts by women who were close to the factory in the beginning and who were able to offer a wealth of wisdom to my research. These accounts are only a sample of the fertile material that many people in the factory and surrounding villages shared with me in 1977, and which were included in the *Tapestry* report.

Grace Ncube lives in Modipane. She was among the first intake of workers to the factory in 1973. A skilled and talented weaver, she produced some of the finest tapestries. She left the Cooperative ten years later and now owns a bar and works her agricultural lands for a living. She is also active in her village, supporting a youth club and a choir.

Diana Meswele is chairperson of the Village Development Committee in Oodi and has been active in village improvement activities for many years. She is a dynamic and energetic woman and has become a major farmer in the area. She brought up her three children who are now working away from home. In 1977, she was facing significant hardship but did not try to get work at the factory.

Itshekeng Molwantwa joined the weavers in 1973 and has been a tapestry weaver for the last decade after doing many of the other tasks in the factory. She also became chair of the Weavers Cooperative in 1996, and is known for her dramatic public speaking abilities.

Grace Ncube

People are ploughing more fields today, but sometimes you think that people who are working [in jobs] are not ploughing. It seems to me that those working are not interested in ploughing. People who are ploughing are those who are not working.

In the past, most people knew that they had to plough; and relatives like uncles, fathers, and mothers could bring all their cattle together and work together. If I had cattle and you had a plough we would plough our fields and then we could plough for money for other people. But today I see other people are not ploughing, but if you ask them why they don't plough they will just tell you that they have no cattle but only a plough. Others will say they have no ploughs. In the past if I had no cattle but I had children, these children would go to you and help to look after cattle then you would plough for me. There is not much of that now. Today agriculture has improved and we have agricultural demonstrators [from the Ministry of Agriculture] but we don't make use of them.

There is water [now] in Matebele and a school and two teachers' quarters. We built the school through *ipelegeng*. But there is development in Oodi only, for there is a tribal office and the Cooperative shop. There is a factory here and they have a policeman and other officers. There is something called Sethunya sa Ditlhabololo and it lends money to people. There was a building contractor here building houses and he borrowed money from Sethunya. But I don't know how this money is lent to people. When we first heard about this money they said [it] could be borrowed by people from Oodi, Modipane, and Matebele. But I have fear only people from Oodi borrowed this money. It was said that when you have borrowed this money there is no interest, so after paying this money back one just continues to make his or her business. But if one comes from Matebele they don't lend this money to him. Oodi people are developing their village because they are given money from Sethunya. In Matebele, houses are falling on us for we are refused the chance of borrowing this money, and we are, therefore, not sharing in this development.

By development, I mean that if you have a donkey cart that is pulled by donkeys and then if you put an engine in it, to me this means that you have developed the donkey cart. It is making life better. And life is better because things are near us. If you are sick there is a health centre in Oodi, and if you are building a house you just go to the Cooperative store here in Oodi. If you want to take your cattle to BMC [the Botswana Meat Corporation] you just bring them here to the Cooperative store.

There are many jobs now also. It is easy to get a job today, unlike in the past. Most people are working in Botswana without going to South Africa. But some don't want to work in Botswana, they want to go to work in South Africa, in the mines where they are given food.

They run away from their homes because if they are here they know that they will have to solve problems of their different homes. Now they leave [the problems] for their wives. Last year after Christmas in January they were told that there were no vacancies at the mines, but they didn't go to Gaborone or Sebele to look for a job, they just stayed here waiting to hear from the mines if there would be vacancies. After a few months they left for the mines.

Even in this factory most of the women are happy because in the meetings you will see that they show an interest, but men are not happy for they just leave the job without giving notice. It was said that there is no money [because of the low June bank balance], so we suggested we should work for one month without salary. The women I could see would work like that, but I don't know about the men. Men could not accept that because they even said that a person who said such things must be mad. Women would work because we think that if we work we will sell something rather than leave the factory to [close].

Perhaps the CUSO people could take it from us for we are owing them. Men do not understand, they think this factory is for women. Yes, we are happy for this factory in our village, for we are able to help in our compounds during the weekends, but men . . . just complain but they don't say so in the meetings. But during the weekends when they are drunk they tell that this is Florida where only women work [Florida is a suburb of Johannesburg where industries employ a high number of women]. They say that they can just leave this "mine of women." You can see that they are not interested because in the last group which finished learning the books [management training] there were no men. There is another group now and there are no men in this group. The only man is Mogapi in the office. There are those who have passed standard seven and they are just like those women, but they refuse to learn anything. They just say, "If we get something to buy tobacco with, it is just okay." If we asked them why they left the job, they just say, "What can we do for there is no money here. . . . I cannot work for nothing when my neck is painful."

Women are working very hard for we are doing everything in our compounds. We are making the courtyards that men are not doing and I have to see if my children are clean. I have to see that the school fees are paid. I buy food and my mind is always working when I think of my children. I don't know if other women are doing the same. Now I think I work harder than their father who is in South Africa at present. Sometimes he writes after three months but even when I read this I don't hear anything that shows we are working together to solve our problems. I am just working as I am always with the children. When they are sick, I am just alone here. After work I have to see that they eat and I must find some wood to cook for them, but where is their father? Women worked even more in the past, for my mother told me that she used to plough carrying me on her back and after ploughing she would cook. What was my father doing? Men just go to the village after ploughing and they don't cook.

My life has improved though, for I got this job [in the village] and I look after my children and property. Before I got a job here my life was very difficult. I had to leave my children with one of the relatives to go and work elsewhere in Botswana, even if I wanted to work near my home. But if one hired me and then said we are going to Kasane I had to go, or if he said I am going to Sikwane, I would also go there. A mother should be near her children all the time for if you are far the old lady who you have left the children with might write you and say the children are sick and you will feel very unhappy so that you might think of leaving the job. Perhaps it is not anything serious.

I say my life has improved because I buy soap and use it for my children and I buy food and eat with my children. I am working for one thing. I started working here having no house to sleep in and now I am trying to build myself a house. I am buying materials with this money. I have a small house now and I want a big one. I also want to dig a field for I have no field now. I want to hire someone to dig a field for me. I had been ploughing but the field did not belong to me. If I ploughed I could get someone to help me plough and someone to take care of my children, for the children will spend the whole day at the fields. Other people are ploughing because they have parents to take care of the fields. If I need more money I can sell beans if I plough for I don't use them a lot. But if I don't plough I could get money from my husband if he sends the money. If he doesn't, I can cook beer and sell it.

I come from a poor family myself; I didn't go to school. I left school for I realized that my young sisters and brothers would die of hunger. So I thought I should go and look for a job. Now I am working and I hire one of my relatives to help me in the compound. Now when school starts I pay for my children and then I can lend this girl money to pay for her sisters. She can pay me later, for her parents stay far away. This is an assistance to them because of my working in this factory. It helps them, because even if one is not working in the factory it means his relative is working there so he can get help from him or her. But this help comes from the factory. I can't just leave my cousin without help when she is sick. If she is sick it means I should take her to the hospital and pay for her, for I know that she is not working and has no money. People can borrow money from me because I am working but they can't borrow from one who is not working for he won't be able to pay.

At first, other people did not want to work in this factory for they didn't know what kind of thing it was. But [now] they want to work here in the factory. There were vacancies [at] the time I came. . . . I didn't wait for my name to be called. I used to come here hoping that perhaps other people who filled in the forms might not turn up and then I could replace their name.

Now [people] realize that we are getting money so they begin to hate us. They see that to go to the factory from Matebele every day will not kill us. Most of them used to say, "Do you mean that you will be able to go to Oodi every day from Matebele?" They even asked us if we were not sick because of walking up and down every day. On the other hand, they are saying that "if I was working I could support my children, I [could buy] a goat or something that I want." We are called those "who are working," and they don't treat us the same as others in the village. If you are a visitor you would be surprised to hear others in the same village being called the factory people. . . . Sometimes if we talk to them they just don't reply to us nicely. This is an insult to us. People are feeling that because we are working we have perhaps to look down on them. But there is nothing like that, it is because they think we are getting money.

There is peace in the factory, though sometimes you can hear that there are those who do not want to work with others when we are doing a tapestry. Now sometimes others refuse to work with the partner she is given. People who were trained first do not want to work with those who came after them, but if you ask why they do that, they say, "You don't know how to knit for you came yesterday, and my tapestry will be bad and get fourth class." I think I am lucky because since I joined this factory I trained first then I worked with Dipugo and she never treated me the way I see other people treating others. We work together cooperatively.

The main problem that I think should be solved in the factory is that of the bonuses. People were working very hard and getting a lot of money; then after a few months we are told that there is no money. We are still owing money for this factory, but if we could do as I suggest things can work out properly. We are in difficulties, for there is no money at the bank to pay us and we are also owing BDC. We are waiting to sell some of our stocks so we can be paid. We were not told directly at the meeting about our account and that there is no money. The management committee has to tell us about their last meeting and we don't know if we should support their decision or not. Those who say they want bonuses will raise their hands and those who do not want bonuses will raise their hands. Perhaps Rra Masiza might say that we have to get bonuses for we don't know what he thought of when he introduced this system of bonuses. They might say that without bonuses we will close.

We now get money according to how good our tapestry is. If the eyes of the person who judges favours your tapestry, then you can get something that can help you. But if you have done something to the person which he doesn't like, then you have lost your money. We are not pleased about the way our things are judged. I think that if we were judges ourselves we could fight one day, for what you like is not what I like. . . . To tell the truth, we don't like this judging. We just want to work for a salary so that one knows exactly how much one gets. It is no good that one month you get P72 and the next month you get P60 and the third you get P40.

We have small problems in the factory, but we are not educated and we cannot speak for ourselves. I find it useless to tell you that we have problems because I am not able to tell you those problems. We only know how to use our hands here, but we cannot use our brains. Even if you think that something is wrong in the factory, you cannot say it out, for if you go to the office they will ask you to explain what you mean and you just say the money is small, but not explaining the reason. We also always say that we don't get enough money but we are working hard. If the person who pays comes with the book and explains the way we are paid, we don't even know what she means. We don't know arithmetic. So there is no use to complain without giving reasons.

Personally I think that we the workers sometimes are the ones who don't want to behave in the factory. You will find that people will just leave the place where they are working. This is not good because it means the work will stop. They do this because there is no one called a foreman, and you must just look after yourselves. Now they changed this so there are people who are responsible for those who come late and other things, so it seems to me that this worries people. This system of saying that one should stay where she works is something new to us. Even those who have young babies are told they should have only one time of feeding them. Now the people are not used to this.

When I started working in this factory, I found that there were people who knew how to make payments to the workers [the book-keepers]. But we didn't know how much we would actually get a month. Those who are making bedspreads would make as many as they wanted for they knew that they would get more money. They [the bookkeepers] tried to teach us how they made payments for more work, but we couldn't get anything out of [their explanation of the wage and bonus calculations]. So this should lead to the formation of a foreman who sees that the job is done. We are working nicely now, for the payment going up and down made people quarrel.

The only thing I am not sure of now is how we own this factory. I tried to ask how the factory could be ours, but the answers were just the same: that after paying the account we own the factory. We were told that we borrowed money from CUSO and so when we sell our [products] part of the money goes to paying CUSO, part for us, and part of the money goes to Sethunya. After paying the CUSO account, then the factory will [belong to] the workers; it will be for us, and I think it is a good thing we own the factory. Well, we will see what happens. I ask those who are on the Board of Directors because it seems they understand better than us. They repeat the same thing, only that the factory will be ours.

Diana Meswele

Since my husband left me there is no one who helps me. I just help myself. I make beer, and I get something from the lands and I can make parties. And with the money from the parties I will not be interested in buying good cloths, but I save this money until ploughing time and then I plough with it. I am helping myself in this way, for I hire a tractor. Nowadays it is better, for I also have a child teaching in Oodi. She has done her Junior Certificate so I can ask her for help. I am also selling eggs.

With the money I get from making parties I reserve it for ploughing, but if this is not enough money, then I kill a goat and sell it. But it is difficult for me to plough for I have no one to help me. I have no husband to handle problems. This year I wish to trade six bags of sorghum (out of about 20) for a cow, so that I may have a cow, perhaps it will bear a calf.

I have many children. I would sell my sorghum but I fear if I sell it all, my children will be left without food. I am not selling it to the shops, for I must remember what our needs are. I know that we eat from the plough (one plants his own food). I need a cow and I need a house, but I have failed to get these things. I need a bed and blanket for I am being killed by the cold. I have many problems but I do not want to tell you about my poverty for you will make me cry, and you cannot go and buy me these things. No one can help me while I am just crying about being poor.

You know, the agricultural demonstrators usually come here. So I tell them to come and plough for me so that I can show them I like nothing else but ploughing, and they can see I am a hard worker. It will be an experiment to show other people how to plough well. But they say everyone would then come to them to do their ploughing. They tell many unnecessary things that I know about. They just waste my time. They say I should use my little money to plough down the soil now. If I do that, then I will not have enough money to plough later. So I find no reason why they always come here and ask me useless questions that don't solve my problems — now you are asking me questions. I told you I need a bed but you can't buy it and bring it to me. Will you bring it?

People today do not cooperate as those of the past. Old people used to drink milk, even if they had no cattle. If you don't have cattle today I can't give you milk, for "the cows are not yours, they are mine," people say. Old people could not separate you [treat one differently than anyone else]. One span of oxen was used by a ward. This span of oxen could plough for everyone in the ward, but now they don't do that. I don't know whether it is because there are no cattle and we plough with tractors. Today you have to rely on yourself.

But in general I think this village is easier now. We are progressing, for we even have roads being made. This shows me we are like Rustenburg and Johannesburg. We will no longer suffer without transport. Now that the road is passing behind my house I can catch any truck that passes. We are having nice days now that many people did not see before they died. God gave us who remained behind the strength to work for ourselves. My husband left me with only one wall but this wall is growing because there is water now. We have the Cooperative store which brings things for us from far places. We are no more going to Gaborone to buy corrugated irons for building, but getting them at the store.

There was no water here before, and you could sleep being hungry for there was no water to cook food with. We used to wash with water, and we saved it in another bucket so that we could make mud with it for building. These days we are in happiness. Since God has given us independence we have done much. There were some who said there were rocks in Oodi which prevented the rain, and they say they don't know who broke this rock so that water should come out. Nevertheless, I realize that it was the white people who have brought us many lives, for they found us here with water very far. They came with their machines and brought water to every house. We can all have water for there are pipes bringing water close to all of us in the village.

This village has been backward for a long time but if things continue and go forward, then this village will improve. I heard that there is a *combi* [a local bus] to take people to Gaborone. This is good to have transport. And the school is expanding. And if one is sick there is no problem of transporting him to the hospital for there are many trucks. We have shops and even a cafe. Even this factory has helped because it makes us help those working and they help us. They are the makers of money and we are the makers of agriculture. They buy sorghum from us and I can borrow money if I need to hire a tractor. Then I pay this person who lent me the money with a bag of sorghum.

We have many dams around here which were dug by the government. It is difficult to get people to do for themselves for they want someone behind them all the time. They want to be pushed. Those who are working for money improve their lives for they are getting money. They can build themselves good houses.

Now work is near for those who want to work. People are no longer going to South Africa to work. We have jobs in our towns and the men are not going to Johannesburg in large numbers as they used to do. I see those people who have been there for a long time now working in Botswana. Most of them have come near their homes.

To raise children means to give them food and educate them so that they can help themselves tomorrow. There is a problem when a child is grown up and not working, for he is going to demand everything from his or her parents. The children of today do not obey their parents. Sometimes I think that perhaps something is wrong with the millet they eat at school because we didn't know this millet during our school days. We are crying about what has happened to our children. I don't know really what is wrong with them. To raise children means to give them food and educate them so that they can help themselves tomorrow.

But life is getting better, for compounds have developed. Now I see that this village has developed. We have this factory that was opened. Those who are working help those who are not working. For example I can go to Grace and borrow money if my child is sick and if Grace does not have food I can give her a bag and she pays me at the end of the month. We help each other. There is a good spirit this way. In Setswana we have to help people of the same ward, and Grace and I come from the same ward. You can't just see one whom you don't know and expect him to help you. Well yes, if perhaps my people cannot help me then I'm sure I cannot die in the wilderness for I can find someone who can help me.

And there are some changes I just don't know about. I don't know very well about the chiefs for example. I heard that chiefs used to call the Regiments to go and work somewhere. Today I don't see things like that. The chiefs have no right to call the Regiments. There is also misunderstanding among the chiefs and their people. The chiefs want to exercise their old powers like calling the Regiments to do something they want them to do, but the people say no. I think it was better for the chiefs to do that in the past, for the people were ploughing more lands which means that if you did go to work for the chief, there was still something for your children.

What I am happy about is that this factory brought water. We were fighting for water. It would not have come without this factory in the village. The very borehole that provided water was owned by a few people and now it is for all of us. We all drink water; even though we pay for it, it doesn't matter. If water is as far as Gaborone you will have to go for it. There was some noise from those who bought the engine for the borehole saying that it and the engine were theirs. I don't know the result of their complaints, but now we are paying P2 a year for water. I have never seen anything else the factory has made. To tell the truth I don't even know it, for I have never gone to see what they are doing there.

I could look for a job there, but the thing is I like ploughing. So I didn't want to give the factory employers problems of asking for permission to go to the fields all the time. I also have goats to look after. I don't want to hire someone to take care of my crops for she might not do as I want and for this reason I might leave the job and go to the lands. I am [eligible] but Rra Masiza explained that if you work in the factory you cannot say, "My goats didn't sleep at home and I am going after them," then the following day say, "My cattle have eaten my crops now." This he said would affect his business and so I thought I was not the right person to work in the factory. I don't think I could benefit anything from this job. I even have children in Gaborone and if they are ill I have to go there right away. And if you hire someone to look after the goats . . . then you will be working for nothing because the money you get will just pay for these people you have hired.

I don't mean to say the factory has not helped people working there. It has helped them for we see that they have built houses for themselves and even those who were poor have now improved. There is a difference, they are building. But you know that in the world there are those people who like to imitate what White people are doing. These people who leave their cattle and go to Johannesburg will find they don't have the cattle when they get back because thieves have stolen them.

Grace [who works at the factory] is ploughing because her mother is still alive and she looks after the fields. She is being supported by her mother. She has money from the factory so she can plough. I will even work for those who are working, for they will pay with money. We aren't so [proud] that we can't work, it doesn't matter. There should be farmers and there should be workers, there should be people who produce food for the workers and the workers will produce the money.

The inheritance of this country is agriculture. We cannot all go to the towns and think that we are developing our country. No! Those who are there have gone to develop the country and we are also developing it through ploughing. What we are ploughing is being taken to the cooperative stores and these people in town eat it. These town people forget that we have worked hard to produce these things. If I was ruling the country, those people who go about in towns doing nothing could be whipped so they could come home and plough. They are now thieves, these people. If we are harvesting and feeding these lazy people, then we must forget about ploughing altogether.

I don't think that to develop is only to work under the White man, for to do that means that you are developing White people and not ourselves. If we all go to White persons' jobs, this country will die. Those people are there because they see tarred roads, but those tarred roads were made through agriculture. It is said that the tributaries of this country are livestock and farming. So there are those who go to the factory and we who remain holding the tail [pushing the country from behind]. Now most people have left the fields and their fields look like forests. This affects development of the country.

Itshekeng Molwantwa

Before this factory, we used to sell sorghum and we used to get about P4 a bag. We couldn't do anything with that money. We sent children to school and the money was gone so that if you had no one to help, you couldn't do anything. But since this industry was built there is a difference because if one has made beer the people who work will go and buy with the money they get. In the past, the beer used to last a week because people had no money to buy it, even if the scale portions were smaller than today. Everything that is made for the party doesn't last the night. They just finish everything, for they have money, and in this way we see life is better. Life was difficult in the past, really. You could have beans and no one to buy, now you get more than P10 a bag, perhaps more, for I haven't sold this year. We used to go to Gaborone and sell these beans with a cup, but now we sell them in the village, and even vegetables.

But people don't want to plough these days, they just want to work. Those who plough are those who liked ploughing even before. But others say they have nothing to use for ploughing, others say they have no seed, others say there is no rain. People were ploughing in the past for they had no other work to do. There were no industries to delay them. I don't mean to say that an industry like this one is delaying us, it is because our minds need money now, for everything is money. It was only after this factory that we saw a bag of sorghum for P10. Now we don't want to plough, we just want the money to buy clothes and look smart.

There are people who are crying in the village that this factory should hire them, but the factory can't hire us all. We want them to work and make money like us. Most of the people think that ploughing is not important. I am working but I plough. Some of the people just stay at home and don't plough but I don't know why. Others run after English jobs and do not plough. If you ask a person why he doesn't plough, he just says, "I also want to work."

If you hire someone to look after your field he thinks you won't give him enough bags or you won't pay him well, or even that you won't treat him the way he treats himself. You might get him but he is perhaps going to stay here being angry, and tell others that Mmantshaba is not a good person to work for. We suffer in order to get people to work the way you want. If you say you have not done well, he says "you are wrong." It was easier in the past because we did not depend much on money. I could just cook porridge and invite people in the village and then they come and helped me harvest. I could also cook beer and they came to help me.

Today if I say help me roof my house, I have beer, they will say, "I know beer, we want money." Well in the past we didn't hire people for a long time, we just hired them for only a day or two. People who come to help in order to drink beer are not difficult, for you have not hired them, they are just helping you. There are people who want money and those who want bags of sorghum. But I don't think one who wants money is reasonable because if you give him P10 and give another one three bags of sorghum, you cheat the first one.

On the whole, the work of women has not changed, it is as difficult as before. From the factory at 4:30 I go to the compound and I stamp the corn. I get the soil for the courtyard. The work of any person does not reduce, but I can say a woman works a lot, more than men. A woman is busy everywhere, in the fields and at the compound. If a man is alone in a compound you might find that there is no wood and the yard is dirty but he just stays. We are looking after cattle in addition to our normal duties. It is just the same as before.

Yes, sometimes men are different, for there are those who can help their wives. But people will say, "Why should you do women's work?" This is wrong because this compound is for us all and we should help each other. Yes there are jobs that men can't do, like cooking or drawing water, but if I am sick you have to do that. These days men are beating their wives. They divorce them in large numbers. I don't know whether it is because marriages are made by the magistrate and we sign without the knowledge of the parents. This is different than the marriage we know for ourselves, for our parents sat down and arranged everything for us. Today the man and the woman don't know the law because they just organize this marriage themselves. Men of the past were better for they taught their children [the customs] before they got married. But if you knew you were wrong and the husband beat you, you couldn't say anything.

We are also failing to observe our taboos. For instance it was a taboo to take the soil during the day that you built your house. And there are trees that you could not cut after ploughing, for if you chopped this tree the old people believe that there would be hail to destroy crops. But today they just do what they want. There are no more taboos. Everything has its own time, and even to dig a field we only dig in winter. The old men say it is not raining like before because there is no taboo. If the iguana is killed but not buried, the wind could come and take all the crops. Young people are not accepting these things but they happen.

It is like today we want to follow what White people do, but we don't know them. We don't know their customs. We just speak English, but we don't know how it started or how we came to speak it. What are its taboos? So we want something that is not our culture. I am surprised that even our old people today don't obey their taboos, for sometimes you find old men chopping the tree, and if you ask him why he does that, he just says, "I can't be lazy and stay without doing something."

The young people are refusing completely. They don't obey these taboos, they don't obey their parents. You might find that when you wake up you find that he or she is not at home and we don't know where they went. He has just gone to Gaborone. We don't know what to teach our children because they don't want to listen to us. If you tell your daughter what happens if in this situation [sexual intercourse and pregnancy], she tells you that she will just buy a tablet, but I don't know who told her about these tablets. From there she goes and you hear that she has thrown a child away, and she won't come home so that we can get a traditional doctor to give her medicines. She won't be good because she does not obey the taboo. A person of that kind is not good for the land and animals. [These will suffer because of the violated taboo.]

Even one who has lost her husband recently will go into the village [to be with men]. She should be given medicine first and stay at home for a year. But today a husband is buried and tomorrow the woman goes to Matebele then the lands and they [the crops] refuse because it is the taboo according to Setswana custom.

The spirit of the Regiment was good, and we all worked when there was a Regiment. If one could not go, we of the same Regiment would go and look for him. Today we are not forced and we don't care to do anything for who will talk to me. Today we see cooperation in members of the committees like the VDC. You find that if the members of the committee are ten, then they are the only ones who do something. The VDC do their work alone, the PTA do their work, the Cooperative members do theirs. The PTA has long called us to make a house for the children to cook in, but we refuse and they did it alone. It is not good to put things on one person who is trying to work for our village (the headman). We must cooperate, but the reason for not cooperating is money. Everything today is money. These years we need money, for things are high [expensive].

Education has changed things. Before if a child had standard two, we knew they could write their name and then left school. Now we want to see that a child should go even where I cannot pay for him. I teach this child because I want him to get more money than what I want. We want education today because education is good, for in the past the inheritance was a cow. Now the inheritance of today is education. We have killed a cow and we have killed the old life and now we are living a new life. We are killing the life of "cattle and sorghum" and we are creating a life of "education and money." The four of them are good if they go together, but we are failing to do that.

When I said develop, I mean to do something that can make our children live better, like schools. We can contribute money to build schools in our home. We must help the chief in thinking what to do for our village — this is cooperation. The chief is the chief by the people. We must help him in everything.

If you call people to the *kgotla* and say let us think of something for our village they won't come, but if you kill an ox they will all come. They just want to be given food and nothing else. If you talk of a school they say our children have long been taught and now that they are at university who is going to work for us. If you talk of a clinic they say, "Since I was born I have never been injected and even my children will never go there." These are the problems, for he thinks that the injection will make him sick. At the office there are policemen and he thinks they will arrest him. He knows nothing about education in schools. He thinks the only useful things are cattle. If you talk of the road he will say, "Where is it going to, the young people should do it for they will use it."

They have not yet realized what is meant by people working for themselves. But when they are drinking beer they complain that there is nothing being done in the village. They say this chief has no work, but if he calls them they say, "What is he calling us for?"

Before this factory we needed water. This well that is giving us water today was dug by Mosadinyana [Queen Elizabeth, the British government]. Then some people from this village felt they would group themselves to buy an engine for this well. Other people refused to contribute money for an engine, so we said we will buy it and the well started operating. While the well was operating, the council came and told us that every well that belonged to Mma Mosadinyana is taken by the council. We of Oodi refused, saying that we had bought everything for this well. They asked us if we had dug it and we said it was given to us so no one can take it. There was a misunderstanding. Lenchwe tried to talk but we couldn't understand while we were still arguing about the well.

The factory arrived so it was easy that the well was taken by the council. We let them take it, and those not affected laughed at us saying that you have lost: "You have long said that this well is yours and now where is your engine you bought?" I think it is good to bring water to the village. We wanted to think of cattle only and forgetting the people in the village. Some of us understood this, but others couldn't understand this. That borehole was for cattle only and we were drinking from the river here.

Some of us didn't work for a White man ever, myself for example. I had never seen a White person, it was my first time to see a White person. That's right! So I asked [my husband] if he would allow me to work here, for I failed to work in South Africa and I wanted to work. Perhaps I would have died without knowing how a White person behaves, whether he behaves just as I behave. I now have seen that a White man does as I do, he is just like me.

They say I am rich but I am not. I have a tractor yes, but it makes me poor, for it breaks down, even a small thing, we will not eat, for it will cost a lot of money. My husband is working but he is paying two taxes, in the Transvaal and here. Now I am helping him by paying school fees for the children. People think that we are rich because our compound is a compound of ploughing. We plough every year but we can't get out what we hope, only five or ten bags, and that is why they call us rich. But we are both working and there is not proper care of the fields. Should we have people to help us, we would be ploughing many fields. But he should not eat the saliva of his comrades, for if one helps you it is because God has given you that fortune.

I like working in this factory, and I want the money to grow, for it is not enough now to support the whole family. I give my children my money and the tractor even. I even have to borrow sometimes from other people. This money is not enough for me, but no one on earth has ever said "I have enough money." When we closed [the factory] last year we said that we wanted our bonuses to make sure that this industry is ours, for we can't believe without seeing anything done for us. We were given the bonuses; I got P93 but I did nothing with this money. Even when I can get P200 I would say it would be better to get P300.

We were told this industry is yours but we don't understand. We don't even understand why they say there is no money to pay us this month. We just say yes, without understanding. We think Rra Masiza is holding us with our heads [deceiving or playing tricks] to say that the industry is ours. It is his factory. But I personally believe that the industry is ours. With those bonuses we can develop our village. Rra Masiza talked a lot about making a place where children can be taken care of. "You should hire people who will take care of your children. Your children should not suffer while you are working," he said. We refused this idea [but] we will think of that after.

We can do something with the other bonuses that we will make. This is money for our village. Those in the village do not believe that this money is also theirs, they say it is ours [the factory workers]. Those in the village think that the factory is for Rra Masiza. Those who understand know that the factory is for both the workers and the non-workers. This factory is for our village and we develop our buildings with this money.

But there is going to be misunderstanding after the departure of Rra Masiza, for everyone is going to want to be in a high position in the factory. We will want to work in the office. You will find that perhaps one in the office has not passed the standard I have passed at school; then I am going to say this person cannot get the same money that I get for she is not of the same education. She is going to say this factory is hers so she should get what everyone gets regardless of education.

We are not in a position to run this factory ourselves. The government should find us a person who will run this factory. There is still a lack of cooperation among the workers. For instance, if we happen to call a meeting without Rra Masiza present, it is always a lot of noise, but if he is present, things work out okay. If it is only us, we just leave the meeting without knowing what we wanted to talk about. But if he is present, because he is a White man, things go all right. We could be starting to cooperate while he is still here to show that we can run it by ourselves. These small things that people say to others are not good in an industry like this one. These small criticisms among the workers give birth to discouragement in the other workers. We cannot run this factory because of this reason. I don't see how we can run it. When [Peder] leaves then it will fall off. We have tried to stop him from going but he refuses. He told us that if we have no minds, we just depend on begging but can't do anything for ourselves.

We can start another industry with these bonuses. We can even make a factory for jerseys. But for this factory to work properly there should be someone from outside our village to run it. We want someone, either Black or White to run the factory. If Chief Lenchwe or the district commissioner can come, we are going to work nicely. We, the people of Oodi, Matebele, and Modipane alone, cannot run the factory.

We don't know where the dye is from, we don't know how the wool is ordered, but he thinks that we can run the factory. How? He should be teaching us these things while he is still here. He just started teaching after we told him that we can't do anything if he can't teach us. He divided us into groups saying that if I teach you all at the same time you don't listen. So if you are in small groups you can ask me questions if you don't understand. If one asks in a large group she is criticized by others so this makes others shy to ask questions. So he taught us how to keep the books and others were taught how to mix the dye. Before he used to do everything from mixing the dye to the books.

We could manage to run this factory if there was no hatred. Sometimes we say that the manager [Mogapi] is not doing good but we can't tell him about this. Ours is just to gossip in corners about him. If you have something to ask, others pass bad remarks about you. We are fearing to ask questions. If you say this blanket is not good, one will just say you have not made it so you better leave it alone. We are just saying everything is beautiful even though you see that it is not, just to please the person who made it. So we are going to pull each other here and there. We are going to tell those who are given the responsibility of judging that they have long been giving their friends first class while their things were not that good to be given first class.

It is good that the factory is ours also for it will work for the villages, but if someone can come from outside and own it then Sethunya will die. He will sell things and put the money in his pocket. If it is ours, we give our bonuses to Sethunya to develop our village. We don't want someone who will hire us and get all the money for his compound. In this way we won't benefit from the factory. We want someone to run it for us, not to own it.

These English jobs are difficult for us to know. They are trying to teach us but we have not got anything by now. Even when you ask me what colours can you mix in order to get the right colour, I just don't know. If you say there is no money we do not believe that there is no money, we don't know what they mean by saying that. We always see Mokgatla carrying things to send away when they say our things are going to be shown at the shows and they do not come back. Whether they come, we don't ask. These are heavy problems.

Rra Masiza left us sometimes when he was sick, but because everything was ordered we did well even without him. Even the things not ordered our manager Mokgatla was able to order. We choose our own stories and knit them. When he came back he was so happy that we had been running the factory well. We did this knowing that the White man will come back so if we can't work well our manager is going to report us when he comes back that we were not working. If we knew that he is gone for good, we are not going to do the work properly.

I know our job doesn't need education, for we were told that as long as you can do what you are asked to do, you would be all right. But I think at this moment, we need somebody who is educated to keep our books and be able to order and send out parcels. We need one who can explain everything fully to us. We need such a person, yes. We also need those who are not educated but have a brain to use in their work and also be brave to ask questions. One who is not educated can see things that an educated person may not see. We need cooperation, that's all. We want people like Mokgatla who have the light but we don't want many of them for they can cheat us.

Rra Masiza writes English and Setswana while Mogkatla is explaining in Setswana. A few weeks ago he told us that he wants to teach us from standard one, those who have never been to school. He also wanted to teach us drawing but no one accepted that, for we want money, we couldn't waste time and money with drawing. We don't regard this as something that can help us tomorrow, even to be able to run our factory on our own. If he says something that can help us we think that he is trying to make us lose.

I don't know about the bonuses though, for I have been paid with bonuses. I am doing spinning and it is hard work because if you can't go to work it means you have no money. We are working on scales [by weight of spun wool] and if I have many scales then I get money.

Chapter 5

Results and Reflections 1997

A formal evaluation of the firm (as done in 1977) did not take place in 1997. It is, therefore, not possible to go into extensive detail about the workers' current views of the Cooperative. However, in this chapter, we can provide some general feedback from the workers and, specifically, from individuals who have known the project since it began. We are also including a short section on how the women in particular have benefited from their participation in the Cooperative, since this is an important element of what the Oodi Weavers Cooperative has accomplished.

The Cooperative Members

The weavers met in March 1998 to examine a draft manuscript of this book and to offer their opinions, which Keitseope documented. When the weavers were asked for their assessment of the factory's success or impact, they were quick to give it a complete thumbs up. Obviously, the weavers who commented were a biased selection of workers, since other weavers who did not find the Cooperative rewarding have left for other pursuits. However, when asked to explain what the Cooperative has meant for them and their community they were able to substantiate their opinions. Keitseope wrote the following section after this meeting.

* * *

In reviewing the past, older weavers who have been with the firm since its inception recognized that major changes have occurred since the firm started. They noted both quantitative and qualitative changes in the areas of social and physical infrastructure, government and donor assistance programmes, as well as production and the income generated by the firm. These changes have led to substantial improvements in their social and economic lives, they said. The weavers identified two key issues as particularly critical to determining the success in their firm: the physical growth of the firm and social benefits derived from such growth.

Physically the firm has grown very big. It now accommodates about 35 weavers at a time. With a lot of support from outside the country the building has been painted, it is well equipped with tapestries, and currently electricity is being installed. All of the weavers were happy about social benefits they derived from the firm. Even new members were happy because they felt that their lives improved since joining. It is far better than staying home the whole day and doing nothing, they said. Weavers in general were very poor and their lives have improved since joining the firm. Now they are able to build houses, feed members of the family (we are "no longer beggars"), plough, send children to school, and buy household furniture and appliances. Overall, family, community, and social life have improved and they are very happy.

But it was also noted that these changes have come about in a highly paternalistic and patronizing manner, and, therefore, the success achieved has left the weavers in a dependent state with little confidence to carry on on their own.

Weavers recognized the knowledge, skills, and general education they received from the firm as key to the development and growth of the firm. They acknowledged that the skills and general education they have acquired have become the gateway to personal, household, and community progress and better living standards.

On a personal level their confidence increased as a result of exposure to and working with other people. About 85 per cent of the weavers said that before joining the firm they were very timid and could not speak in front of other people, but now through interaction with others they have managed to improve their self-esteem. Some of them were frightened since they had never met a White person before, for example.

They also felt their firm has been a success in the sense that they have the blessing of visitors from all over the world. The international image of the firm gives them pride. As one of the weavers put it, "Just visit any part of the world where White people come from, and you will find our village-life products, and thus Oodi Weavers is travelling the world." They were very happy that every time visitors come to Botswana they are sent by the government to visit the factory.

Overall, the weavers expressed personal satisfaction with what they are getting from their firm, no matter how humble. As one of the women put it, "I grew up in this firm; if it were not for it I would be finished, I would not have my little goats or chickens. I cannot leave now because I am still taking care of my grandchildren."

* * *

A Perspective on Gender*

The weavers' project did not consciously begin as a "women's project," but it has virtually become one. The original project proposal does not feature women, but it does acknowledge the disadvantaged position women hold in Botswana society. The weavers do not necessarily refer to themselves as a women's cooperative, but in most discussions we had with other people in Botswana there was a repeated and general reference to the women of the factory, though men are also involved.

The question many observers ask is, "How has the project affected the women in particular?"

There is a vast literature on how to identify gender issues or benefits in development projects, and some include criteria that can be used to judge the value of CED activities for women. For our purposes we have used *Two Halves Make a Whole: Balancing Gender Relations in Development*, published by the Canadian Council for International Cooperation and MATCH International Centre (Moffat, Geadah and Stuart 1991). This compilation of analysis and of evaluation and training guidelines presents an extensive array of questions that can help determine the level of participation, control, and benefit

---

* This section on gender is admittedly very brief for such an important aspect of the weavers' experience. I felt unqualified for a major analysis of gender. Others are competently writing on this subject, and as many people have said, this topic deserves independent study in which the weavers can fully participate.

that both women (in particular) and men can achieve in development projects.

For example, the authors pose the following questions to measure development project outcomes for women:

1. Do women receive a fair share, relative to men, of the benefits arising from the project?
2. Does the project redress a previous unequal sharing of benefits?
3. Does the project give women increased control over material resources, better access to credit and other opportunities, and more control over the benefits resulting from their productive efforts?
4. What are the (likely) long-term effects in terms of women's increased ability to take charge of their own lives, understand their situation and the difficulties they face, and to take collective action to solve problems? (Moffat, Geadah and Stuart 1991, 38)

Tangible and Personal Gains

In terms of the first two criteria above, the Cooperative has clearly and disproportionately benefited women. The Cooperative does benefit more women than men, though through family ties and village participation men are also definite beneficiaries. The women have economic resources and social status they did not have before Oodi Weavers. They operate collectively and, through the ownership of the Cooperative, they have a group support and rapport which they also value.

Economically the women have gained extensively from the Cooperative. They earn a steady wage, which, though small by national standards, is significant when they are able to work in their home villages. With this wage they have built homes, raised families, and expanded their agricultural lands.

Equally important, they are able to maintain their independence and provide for their old age, which they said was very important to them. Also, the wage and the status of working in the Cooperative have enhanced their positions in their families and within the village politic.

These are concrete results gained from the factory that the women themselves have recognized. *Two Halves Make a Whole* also discusses some of the specific power issues and more nebulous relationships that contribute to a successful development venture — those factors that lead to long-term increased control and other non-material benefits (points 3 and 4 above).

In dealing with empowerment and control, the authors simply but thoroughly expand on what is involved:

Behind most attempts to increase women's power was the notion that power is a limited quantity: If you have more, I have less; if I have power over you, increasing your power comes at the expense of mine. This power is an either/or relationship of domination/subordination or "power-over." It is ultimately based on socially sanctioned threats of violence and intimidation, invites active and passive resistance, and requires constant vigilance to maintain.

There are alternatives. We can conceive of power as "power-to," power which is creative and enabling, the essence of the individual aspect of empowerment. Most people describe situations where they felt powerful as those in which they solved a problem, understood how something works or learned a skill.

Collectively, people feel empowered through being organized and united by a common purpose or common understanding. "Power-with" involves a sense of the whole being greater than the sum of the individuals, especially when the group tackles problems together.

Yet another kind of power is "power-within," the spiritual strength and uniqueness that reside in each of us and make us truly human. Its basis is self-acceptance and self-respect which extend, in turn, to respect for and acceptance of others as equals. (Moffat, Geadah and Stuart 1991, 19)

Michael Kaufman and Haroldo Dilla Alfonso analyse the depth to which power and gender are rooted in societies and, therefore, the complexities involved in community development initiatives.

Power is understood as the capacity of certain humans to control and dominate other humans and control social and natural resources. Such a conception of power is not simply a matter of ideology but is the organizing principle that is embedded in a vast range of political, social and economic relations. While it shapes the capacity of all humans to participate, men's capacities to exercise power in this form have been less limited than women's. Nevertheless, as we shall see, men's own capacities for participation are distorted and limited through this process. In other words, differential participation negatively affects men as well as women, although differentially of course, and in most cases, not as severely. (Kaufman and Dilla Alfonso 1997, 154)

The weavers have clearly expanded the influence they have over their lives, at all of the above levels to some degree, based on their experience and relationship to the factory. They spoke of being able to make choices in what they bought and did with their incomes. They felt enabled to determine where they lived — in their home villages rather than being forced to work in Gaborone. While much of this perspective relates to having "power-over" their material existence, it also shows how the women can have the "power-to" determine more aspects of their lives.

Many of the women also spoke about the importance of their personal growth and changes, the "power-within" themselves that they developed through participation in the Cooperative.

As Dr. Kgomotso Mogome-Ntsatsi observed from her research on community development and conversations with the weavers, they demonstrate important confidence, articulation, and social awareness, as individuals and as a group, which she attributed to their Cooperative experience.

> What strikes one immediately about this group from the factory is the way people are willing to assist themselves more. From a state of helplessness they suddenly see possibilities of rising higher and influencing others to do the same. It would seem that if you give a person the opportunity of meeting basic needs you are also giving him/her the opportunity of spreading her wings sideways to reach beyond self and the nuclear family to the larger community around. There seems to be a great sense of personal worth in the cases we have just looked at and a feeling of fulfillment in having managed to assist others. (Mogome-Ntsatsi 1989, 302)

Limits and Liabilities

However, it is also evident that the women continue to experience severe restraints on their lives, since they have not been empowered to the extent they desire or to the extent that many of their supporters would seek on their behalf. Their income from the Cooperative is below standard, and the ongoing existence of the factory is far from ensured. They still struggle with daily problems of the factory that reduce the overall security and pleasure of working. Though our interviews with the women did not deal with their domestic and personal lives, it is evident they do not have a great deal of personal security and independence. And like many other women in the village, the weavers are still burdened by the simultaneous responsibilities of household demands, tilling agricultural lands, caring for children, and often performing the duties of wives in addition to being daily workers at the Cooperative.

In *Gender Roles in Development Projects*, Maryanne Dulansey and James Austin write about the importance of women's involvement in economic development of this type.

> Small-scale enterprise [SSE] is particularly important for women who need to earn income. It is more flexible and less restrictive than employment in larger enterprises, which may require education, training, and/or experience that women lack; such jobs may also require that work be done at times and in places that are culturally unacceptable or difficult for

women with family responsibilities. SSEs can be built upon knowledge and skills women acquire in the family, can be engaged in part time and within the household if desired, and can facilitate the transition from agricultural employment as it begins to decline. (Dulansey and Austin 1985, 80–81)

However, additional barriers that women can experience in these enterprises are evident in the weavers' case. "Social attitudes concerning women's value, abilities, and proper roles, often internalized by women themselves, are the single most serious barrier to women's entry and success in small-scale enterprises. The combination of these negative attitudes with women's commitments to raising a family further intensifies and strengthens the barrier" (Dulansey and Austin 1985, 106).

Juggling Responsibilities

The women at Oodi Weavers continue to juggle the competing forces of traditional versus modern roles and rules that define who they are, what they can or should do, and how they can affect change in their lives. The women have adapted to a workplace culture that they were unfamiliar with, and that requires new forms of cooperation, decision making, and individual discipline. At times their experience and knowledge of conventional social relations have supported them as workers, for example, in building the personal bonds that sustained cooperation requires. Conversely, they have also tried to integrate what they have learned at the workplace into their personal lives. But they often rely on traditional roles, such as the dominant male authority in decision making, which has limited their ability to manage production and deal with organizational issues. For instance, one close observer of social relations in Oodi noted that the weavers seem to be more judgemental towards and often more abusive of women in management positions than of men.

As members of a CED enterprise, the women have had some impact on the economic and social life of Oodi and neighbouring villages and, therefore, they can contribute to the potential for sustained development of their community. Though difficult to measure, they have created an aura of possibility and potential within a social context of change, which contributes to what others are doing to better their lives and the overall condition of their village. Their existence demonstrates initiative and innovation. The village leadership, for example, was clearly concerned about the viability of the Cooperative as they considered its presence as both an economic and inspirational asset.

However, as women, the weavers are not accorded equal status to men in village *kgotla* decision making processes — men still dominate the political and economic elite. For example, there were paternalistic overtones in the way some of the village leadership treated the weavers in meetings we attended. And while many of the weavers are now respected members of major village institutions, such as the Village Development Committee and Secondary School Board, women in general do not constitute equal numbers and they do not have equal status in the village authoritative hierarchy.

The women of Oodi Weavers are thus left in a precarious state, constantly contending with the gender limits imposed on them (and all women) by their culture, yet experiencing a new authority as workers and as women in their workplace. They are creating a daily balance between retaining old and creating new cultural behaviour as they chart new courses through the practical matters facing them every day.

Three Women Speak

Many of the people who were interviewed for the 1977 report are no longer in Oodi. However, three women who were interviewed (quoted at length in chapter 4) were available in 1997 and were most willing to speak about the Cooperative again. A summary of these conversations, which reflect a diversity of experience with the Cooperative (post-membership, village connection, and continuing member) are reported here.

Grace Ncube

I stopped working at the firm a long time ago, I forget when exactly. I liked it there. I had to look after my children, though, and I had no one to help me then. No one to help me with my lands.

Even though I am not doing that kind of work at the Oodi Weavers, I know that if I find time there are things I can do that are similar to what I did at the factory. I learnt a lot at the factory when I was there. While continuing with my business I can do other things, like weaving small tapestries to make a profit.

I tried to find new workers to replace me but the firm said there were no places available. I had thought of going back but there was a period in which we could come back if we wanted to, but for me that time had passed.

If some say the wages were not enough at the firm, I don't believe that could be the problem for them to leave. When we compare that to the fact that you can be close to home to do your duties, the money is enough so that you can be near your home. Some of the men were feeling bad when Rra Masiza was here. At the firm, for the men to be employed it took some time to explain the structures and, therefore, why there was the idea of men feeling bad about working with women, but this was gradually reduced. I am missing what I did at the firm but if I was to start weaving tapestries in my home it would take only two months to get back to the quality I was producing.

I have a good relationship with the workers. I sometimes visit them in the firm. We see each other except when other things like village commitments keep us busy on weekends. For example, funerals, weddings, *kgotla* meetings, and village societies keep us busy. No, they never visit me at my home, the people from the firm. But the reason they don't visit me is a minor one. One person can see that I have a talent but another person cannot agree that I have that talent. There is some resentment. That is why the firm was not doing well, because people were not allowed to share their ideas.

But I don't know what the main problems were at the factory in the last few years. If you ask those who are working, they will say something surprising, like they ran short of material and they did not have anything to sell, or that they did not have money or the firm was in debt. So I realized that they cannot manage. If you are in business you must have a good stock, and they should have called the former weavers to help. Now that the firm is owned by the present owners, the management committee must take their own decisions and then tell the members of the firm and reach agreement to seek advice from other people outside the firm. If they just keep quiet, we fear to intervene because we won't know when they need our help. I would have come to help if they called me, without a hesitation. I have not heard from them ever.

Also I have been thinking of asking them if they send out application forms for employment. They say yes, but they then say they don't have money for training new people. I used to tell people that anyone could come to find a job at the firm and that it is important to work in the village. Even now I wish other companies could come and invest in the village. Because we are suffering while our children go to the towns to look for jobs, and when they work there, they have additional costs of transport and rent, so they do not have a lot left at the end of each month.

This kind of project would be good for Modipane. The problem is that business is slow in the village. Even those who are interested in opening a business would be discouraged because of the bad road, because it is difficult to take things to town and back. For myself I have similar problems, no transport. I don't know if the road will be improved. We talked about that many years before but we are promised that it will be improved. People may be interested in staying in the village if the road is improved.

The factory is the only thing that can help, the only firm in Botswana that we are proud of. I heard that in the schools they teach about it, and on the radio they talk about the weavers. If it was doing very well it could help more of the people.

The thing is that the people who are working there can buy the products from us who are ploughing — eggs, vegetables, beans, milk, and sorghum. Life would be smooth if jobs were created in the village. If I had someone to help me with my lands it would be easier to also have a job. This village is a combination of lands and village, so the good thing is to plough and take good care of your fields. I think it is very important for those who are working to also plough. If you are just working without ploughing, life will be difficult for you. Money cannot be relied on alone.

There is a shortage of land, though, as many lots have been taken. We have told the chief that it is a good thing that many people are coming from outside, but what worries us is they don't care about what is important in the village. They just ignore us. They just concentrate on their jobs in Gaborone, coming back in the evenings, not attending *kgotla* meetings and not taking part in village activities. Some developments are planned taking into consideration the numbers of people or voters in a village, but even then the outsiders are not really counted as part of the village. They don't attend funerals. There is nowhere they can help in the village. The village helps them get a plot but we get nothing in return. The responsibility for this is with the chief, who signs the applications for the Land Board. He is the only person who can call them to do something for the village.

I think the developments you see in the village are useful but when you look ahead you won't know if people see things with a good balance, since the towns are being built up but not linked to where the people are living. Nowhere is there an effort to help those people in agriculture, though we rely on agriculture as a nation. I wonder if they are going to manage, or if agriculture will survive. There are lands just on the edge of the village but the government says they will take them away. They don't give us new plots for our lands. I just plough but I don't have my own fields because it is near the village, and I was warned that it will be taken at any time. I don't know where to move to.

The other problem we are having in many Motswana villages is the youth unemployment. Our children who did not do well in school are not going on in school. They are not interested in agriculture or in working and, therefore, they are just at home doing nothing. I appeal to people like you to counsel them. I sometimes stand up at the *kgotla* and say that we have a problem with the children roaming the streets. They drink alcohol before their time, smoke, and even become parents too young. I suggest you meet VDC members to discuss the problems of the youth and those who are jobless.

Those children who pass their examinations will have a better life because in Botswana to get employment you have to be academically fit or have work experience for a job. So for those who are ignorant like myself, we will find it difficult. Since I am an old person I think I am much better off than those who work in the towns, who stay in a big house but pay a rent for it. If you lose your job and you don't have a plot it will be a major problem. In my case it is better to stay at home and work in the fields and not have money but I don't pay for rent, electricity, or water.

The factory can help because in a village it will be like bringing employment to the people. So you can work at your home. But the firm does not encourage people in the village any more. While Rra Masiza was there, tapestries were brought to Matebele and Modipane, but after he left the weavers did not continue to let others see the tapestries. Nobody comes here, not to Modipane. And we did not give samples of the weaving to the clinic or the school. We did give one to the university. The people in the villages only know that the firm exists and that it can give some employment. But they don't know what procedures are used there, even I don't know now. I left a long time ago so I don't know what changes there are.

People know what is sold there. The problem could be that it is difficult for Batswana to buy expensive tapestries. That is their main problem. Even the villagers who are wealthy enough to buy tapestries are not well informed about what is being sold there — they just see the buildings.

Diana Meswele

The firm helps the people of the village; actually it helps alleviate poverty. [The workers] don't have to go out of the village to find jobs. So those who are working there will help others who are not working. Because our children are working. Even if there is a village activity, for example, something sponsored by the VDC, they will take part in it. Look at these photos [of a recent event at the factory]; they will show our unity with the people from Oodi Weavers. It was a farewell party organized for Mrs. Hoff, the Peace Corps volunteer who was at the factory. She did a great thing for us. She helped get the firm on its feet after it collapsed.

The factory is useful also for people in the village, for those who worked at the factory, they have started small businesses. It has been a kind of school; the workers have learnt something. They have gone to apply for FAP loans [Financial Assistance Programme — a government loan system for entrepreneurs] to do something for themselves.

Before [Mrs. Hoff] arrived, it was very difficult at the factory. We tried to see what could be done. We considered closing the firm completely, but we invited almost anyone to help and that is how she came. When she first came she knew nothing of the firm, but she showed us how businesses work and she invited many people from her country, and this helped the firm stand up again. If these people did not come we could be crying now. Even the workers were leaving, only a few remained. I think things will be okay now that they have the expert there [the Japanese volunteer]. Even the salaries are better now because sales have improved.

There is cooperation between the VDC and the firm. For example, at the party for the National Service students tomorrow there will be gifts from the village. The weavers gave money for these. We visit them also. We work together and help each other; this is the unity I talk about. I want you to come tomorrow to see this unity.

It is true, though, that we still have some problems in our village. We have problems with those who come to take plots here, those foreign people. They don't come to funerals or weddings, though they are around. I for one think the chief has to prove to them that he is chief and that they should contribute, if we have fundraising, for example. There are those outsiders who are cooperating, so it is only some who do not contribute, who don't participate. They just ignore us if we knock at their door. The chief has energy to show them what to do, he has the power.

There are many developments here now but some have brought some problems also. Our children are crooks or *tsotsies* [a term used in South Africa for young street thugs]. They, the children, came up with these developments, developments that we don't like. The youth nowadays don't want to work, they just want to do house breaking. They go to school to learn how to steal from people, without wanting to find employment. Some of these leave good or rich homes to live on the streets in Gaborone, where they join criminal groups. That is why we want to bring a Brigade here, so that if we see these youth we can reform them, so they don't engage in these bad activities but can earn their own vegetables. We need some employment for these young people instead of letting them spoil the good name of our country.

We went to Mochudi (the district capital) to contact the Brigade people about starting a Brigade here. It will be a multi-purpose Brigade as our children are not doing well, so part of the Brigade will be for building construction while others learn cooking or sewing — different things our children can do. We are concerned about the prospect of no jobs for our youth. We met with representatives of other villages and we had one opinion — the problem of our youth. We resolved that the Brigade should be near us so that the youth should benefit from it, instead of going far away. Now they just seem to roam the streets.

We have another problem, as the VDC, that people are not cooperating with us, when we have activities we just keep inviting them to. For example, when we are molding bricks, only a few will come to help. We are working hard as everything is on us now. Yesterday I came from the lands to prepare for the *kgotla*, and tomorrow I have some other duties. We are just volunteers on the VDC and that is not good.

Some of the people in the village do not understand, some of us are typical Batswana, they just want the old ways. They think we are being paid in the committee, paid a lot, but we are just volunteers. This shows a lack of understanding, but they cannot be blamed for ignorance. For those of us who volunteer, who are committed, though we have very little education it shows that we love this village. Even if we are losing [personal income] we are still standing for the village. My goats could be eaten by a jackal while I'm here because I don't go out enough with them but I am committed to my village.

These years and all the work have made me suffer, but I like the committee and if I am voted off the committee I will continue as a volunteer to help them, so I can share my experience with this and that development. We have not been lazy. Some people are just the same but they don't have the same views about the village. Some people will refuse to help certain people, because it will make them rich or they will not volunteer. Others are good people and they have some useful expertise.

But some people are jealous, that is why some people hide from

God as some are serpents, they just say we don't have expertise in the *kgotla*. They don't think we women can stand up and say things in the *kgotla*. Because some stand up to say nothing useful. God gave us ideas and if we do not contribute these ideas because we fear people will say bad things about us, we will be anxious.

I just have a good spirit of building my nation, a spirit of love. If there is a *kgotla* meeting I just tell people to come. I say that the chief is the servant of the government, and they should come to hear what the chief says so that we can do what we should do. Only, some are discouraging, as they say they cannot neglect their goats. I don't have that spirit. I can get more to come to the *kgotla* by talking to people eye to eye, but we never fill the *kgotla* now. We still hear the excuses. The country is changing. When some Indians wanted to help us — and they sent a message that they would bring food to the *kgotla*, a big meal — then all the people came. Many came as there was food, but this was a different thing.

Itshekeng Molwantwa

Things in the firm are going well now, yes, things are okay now. What we are lacking, though, all of us, is to plan ahead. We don't plan ahead. So if we have a stock, and if we have to deliver it far, we refuse, because "it is too far"; we say, "Who will look after my children while I am away?" I don't say I'm on duty and must do my share. I don't say I'm being sent away by my company. I only think of my family matters, not the firm. We just waste time protesting. Another example. When we talked about money yesterday, people only spoke up when they thought they are being cheated, which shows we don't know these things, how to deal with money and to plan. We cannot go to a distant place, like Francistown, on business, as some will just refuse. Then we all refuse and we just argue among ourselves. We should plan ahead and go everywhere. To go out in this way, we will be selling more.

The Cooperatives people help us by doing our books, to make sure our group is going along well. Second, they help us with management, as we don't have the management that sees into the future, so that when the volunteers came they could work with us and help us. The Cooperatives helped us get the volunteers, and when this one [Setsuko Takazawa] leaves they will send another. Yes, they also help us with training, as you see with Josephina and Thebe, who just went away for a week of training, free of charge. But we have to pay Thebe while she is at Sebele [Cooperative Training Centre]. She went so she could carry out our duties perfectly. We have been working with them for many years.

The Cooperatives came and they brought two tutors, and they would take a week teaching, cooking food, while we continue with a course, if I can call it a course. They view us as just okay because they take our books and see that we are okay, otherwise they would say they are unhappy. Sometimes it is that we feel we are not doing the proper accounts. Mr. Mogotsi [from the Cooperative Department] came once, and he tried to correct our system of wages, but we refused as we could not understand his way. He wanted to raise the square metre limit but we were against that. We said we could not do that because it was too much work. He wanted to change everything except the basic salary. What he wanted to set was too much, higher than we could reach. We knew we would fail to reach that limit, though some of us were reaching that limit already.

We were helping ourselves and they would give this opinion, but if we don't like what they say we would oppose them in their presence. We knew if we tried to increase production we would just struggle and not do a good job; we'd spoil everything trying to speed our work. We were called a "factory of failures" [because of the poor quality of materials from 1990 to 1994], and people still ask if we are producing like we did before. When we struggled to reach Mr. Mogatsi's limit, we were not doing well and our sales decreased. Those of us who wanted to work to improve sales could not even make his limit.

When we were having problems, they [the Cooperative agents] worked with us; they tried to advise us, they said the problem was that we were not producing because we were not [following Cooperative rules]. They said we were hard to supervise and that we did not take our work seriously. They said we collapsed because we were not taking good care of ourselves. For example, some said Josephina knows us, is part of our family, and therefore no one could retrench [fire] anyone. We wanted people to retire by themselves, not to be told to retire. That showed we were not taking care of ourselves. And then we started to be playful; for example, we would just go to the cooking place to avoid work, to play around. Even if someone tried to reprimand us we would continue to play around so our production was very low, until some of the other weavers who had left came back. So some of us retired and only a handful remained.

Those who remained knew the Cooperative was theirs, and despite the things they were against, despite those difficult things, the group acted like the *kgotla* [together]. And then we put the stick to ourselves [self-encouragement] and stayed behind without being paid. I think this continued for about five months that we worked without being paid. We knew that Gowenius gave the factory to us.

He told us that we bought this firm with our hands. And we realized that this very place was something we have to die for, so that it will be retained for our children. When our children grow, maybe they will remove these rafters and put those that they like, but it will be theirs, for them to inherit. We inherited this place and we must pass it on. And indeed we remained — our lands were there, our husbands were there but they did not say that we should not go to the firm because we are not paid; they knew we had to go because it was our property.

Other weavers have that spirit to show that this firm is ours. We thought we would lose hope when some of the members retired but that was not the case. We remained here so we could see where we would end. We were saving what little [weaving wool] we had and using it sparingly so that the others who left could come back. But some left without their shares and came back, but came back to take us to the Cooperative court for their shares. We told them that if a cooperative collapses you don't get anything, but we who remained decided that they would not lose altogether and that they should get their shares so that we would get our shares when we retire, as this is how cooperatives are for the members.

Yes we have one spirit now because those who retired are back again. They decided to come back and to work very hard. We do not bother them now and though we thought that these people would leave again they have remained. Also we who stayed here decided the others could return, as we would not have to train them again, and they could create more stock for sale straight away. They are working very hard with us now and we don't have to waste time retraining or worrying about paying them their shares.

We have equal shares. Originally we were not equal when the firm was doing well and the shares we were owning had an interest of 20 per cent every year. But when the company collapsed, we changed this. Now we are different. Those who came later do not have the same amount of shares. Everyone knows this. Everyone is trained for a year when they start at the firm and we study her closely for that year before he or she can buy shares. Then she gives us something, like we deduct P20 from wages each month for the shares. The training only takes three months and when she finishes she is okay to start, and we start to pay a salary. So those you hear complaining about wages are all members, and as a member you can say whatever you want. The people who are employed are outside the membership. People are never the same.

We, the older members, have this spirit that the firm is ours but others may feel differently because everyone is different. We are going to fight so that the firm will not collapse while others may not be as concerned if it collapses. Some are feeling that "others say it is ours when it is not." People are not the same. I cannot say I know your mind. Of course you can say something but mean something else. For example, when we remained behind some just left to look for work and we thought they were not as concerned about the firm. We are now back together. To be back does not mean we are going to punish them who left. Now that the firm is on its feet again we are getting something, a little, though as the time goes on, we will get more.

No one gets money from their shares. Every month as I work I get my daily wage and then I deduct my share. I may get my bonus this month or next. But the production bonus we take every month if we meet our measure. At the end of each year we just get our wage, only that. We claim the shares, our money, only when we retire. Once we did a certain programme, gratuities, so each worker could get something more when they retire but this did not materialize, as our company collapsed when we were not producing enough. Since then we realized our work needs many people and that we can only put some small amount aside for ourselves; we must not touch our shares, they must be left for when we retire.

The Cooperatives people are saying "this firm is yours," so they cannot do anything without we the management committee saying so. We [the management committee] sometimes try to say something but others criticize us. We discuss an issue and we submit it to [the membership], but they criticize us and refuse it. No one has a higher position here and no one is being blinded or exploited here.

All of us bought shares and now we have equal shares and we all can give advice, like "this tree should be removed," but when we get to the issue of money and business, they never agree. Sometimes they agree with our suggestions but often they will just criticize and say "this will spoil our work." They will say they want us to bring an issue to them, so they can agree or disagree. For instance, if the people from the Cooperatives want to come to explain things to us, the weavers just refuse, saying this is not how we do things, this organization is ours, even this management committee. "We are equal and we want things this way! They will come if we need to understand something, but this organization is ours!" The Cooperative people will say that the members should listen to us, the management committee, but then they say the committee is not doing its job well and it should be changed.

We remind those who are objecting to the training that they are bringing down the firm. They respond by saying that if one person does not work well the firm does not collapse, so why should we complain. What some members don't want is for us to be ahead of them, to get paid more than them. They just refuse this! They just refuse straight. Like with the different volunteers, the American and the Japanese, we say we want them to be higher than us [paid more] but the distance between us and them should not be a lot. What they usually say is that things were not done properly from the beginning, by grouping those who are finishing off and those working in the office. The difficult situation is this one. This is why we are against the finishers who are getting more when we are struggling so hard to work. The office people work very hard but they are combined with those who work less.

The future of the factory will not be a good one unless we prepare, put everything in order. In my opinion, I don't remember how many groups there are of us, we came at different times, but we want an expert who can take our books, study them, and see how things changed along the way, and then look at the differences in wages and find out why we get different wages. He should ask questions about why some are getting paid more than others, then he would call us together and brief us. He would explain to us all how some came at different times and, therefore, their wages are never equal.

We understand we are weaving, but Thebe and Josephina [who work in the office] are not weaving; though we started at the same time, we do not get as much as they do. This business expert could review these things and put them straight, but this person should not be employed full time, just come for a short period to work on this issue. We don't exactly want a manager who knows weaving, we can help each other doing that. We can try harder, and we know what colours to use and what wool is good. The volunteers know our procedures, but they cannot intervene on wages or tell us to do this or that. We still need someone to come in for this problem. Otherwise we are doing well now.

Chapter **6**

An Outsider's Observations

W hen I started to plan this book, I knew it had to be more than a mere description of what the Oodi Weavers is and what the people have done. The book had to tell a story: a compelling narrative with layers of information, meaning, and emotion. The weavers' story had to include defining moments of change as well as the ongoing abstract relations that make up daily working life. Their story had to include detailed information of what has happened, but it also needed to reflect the nebulous spirit and intuitive wisdom that keeps the Cooperative going. Thus, this story had to be told in the weavers' words, which prevail through the previous chapters. The photographs tell some of their story, too.

It was also important to tell their story from the viewpoint of an outsider and supporter, someone who could situate their efforts in a broad context of global social change. This is not to diminish the importance of their voices and perspectives, but rather to augment their experience so it can be extended to other people interested in international and community development.

The weavers' experience is part of a global phenomenon of people using economic, social, and personal resources to address their collective and individual needs. Daily, we hear and see the dire descriptions of how global economics have destroyed the fabric of societies, of how industry, government policies, and human migrations have destroyed our natural environment. What we often don't hear is what people are doing at the community level to address these serious issues. While we see a lot of the negative changes in the world, we see less of the new strategies and actions that attempt to give *all* people control over their lives, not just a privileged few.

We must repeat the stories of people living in poverty, young people, women, first nations, and disadvantaged people, who are meeting their physical needs and creating meaning in their lives, now and for the future. It is through these accounts that we learn what can be done to address injustices and that we are inspired to act. It is through these accounts that we are stimulated to think of new ways to reach old and new goals, to realize the commonality of human needs around the world, and to maintain the courage and passion needed for sustained, just development.

The CED Prism

In this chapter, I will examine the Weavers Cooperative through the prism of community economic development (CED),* a worldwide movement of localized change. While there are many definitions of CED (note Douglas 1994; Shragge 1997; or Galaway and Hudson 1994), I believe this term is essentially a label for a directed process of helping people who have been marginalized in society, through sustained economic opportunities at the local level. CED activities may vary in many ways, but they all seek some form of social benefit (collective and individual) from self-sustaining resource-generating action.

CED is an alternative strategy to conventional economic development methods. It is relatively new, but it has proven its worth. As Hubert Schmitz wrote about one aspect of CED,

> An unprecedented opportunity has arisen for those concerned with small-scale industry: an opportunity to go on the offensive. . . . Small has not become beautiful everywhere it appears, but it commands more respect

---

* The Weavers are organized as a "workers cooperative" and this structure could have been used to examine the weavers' experience. Many of the characteristics of workers co-ops and CED enterprises are similar; both prioritize collective responsibility and benefit, for example. What distinguishes Oodi Weavers from workers cooperatives are the village development goals the weavers have committed themselves to, and the membership benefits.

and attention than ever it has. In the form of flexible specialization, small-scale industry has proved its economic and technological strength, not in peripheral activities but in the engine room of capitalism; not in times of easy growth but in times of crisis. (Schmitz 1989, 38)

For comparison, privately owned businesses will prioritize commercial growth and profit as prerequisites to providing social services or environmental programmes through taxation. Most western governments translate this dichotomy into sequential policies that favour private sector growth prior to meeting social needs. For CED ventures, social and economic goals are sought simultaneously and, therefore, function interdependently.

This is a simple and strategic understanding of CED used by practitioners of CED, those who work with many different people and often have to collaborate with people whose world views may be significantly different from their own. In other words, definitions are a product of what people do with their understanding, and, in this case, CED is defined according to the alliances and relations that need to be maintained for effective stimulation of local action and change.

An essential characteristic of any CED venture, though, is that the primary beneficiaries of these ventures are, or will be, the main agents; that is, the groups of people who work in these ventures should control them. For sustained success of a CED venture, therefore, the beneficiaries must acquire new skills, knowledge, and authority that can be exercised within and beyond the limits of the particular venture.

Thus, the participants in a CED activity should have a stake in it, a strong reason to be involved, and something either to gain from the success of it or to lose from its failure. As one weaver said to me, "We are not going to let the firm collapse, because it has given me benefit and it must be here for my children." In other words, she needed and wanted the firm to succeed, not only for her immediate financial benefit but also because she sees a long-term benefit for her family and, by implication, for her community.

Strategic Vision and Action

The CED method is a strategic way of meeting the needs of people who live in poverty but who want to change their economic conditions. They can empower themselves to achieve an element of control over their lives and, thus, enhance their quality of life and the life possibilities of their children. CED works as an anti-poverty strategy because it takes into consideration the psychological, social, political, and economic needs of poor people. As well, the CED model seeks to use and develop community resources that have the potential for sustained long-term support, unlike government programmes, for example, that tend to be project or short-term results driven.

Dal Brodhead outlines a set of characteristics for a CED initiative that we can use to show how the weavers are a part of this phenomenon. He notes that some, or preferably most, of the following goals should characterize a CED initiative, policy, or organization:

- respond to, or emerge from, underdevelopment and marginalization at the community level;
- pursue economic development as a way of empowering people and increasing local self-reliance;
- seek to build local capacity to plan, design, control, manage, and evaluate initiatives aimed at revitalizing the community;
- incorporate a comprehensive development approach that aims to link economic, social, cultural, environmental, and other sectors of the community;
- be inclusive (not exclusive) in its outreach, enabling disadvantaged and disempowered groups in the community to create partnerships with others interested in a sustainable future for the community;
- favour medium and longer-term approaches over short-term quick fixes;
- ensure that benefits accrue directly to the community at large rather than primarily to individuals in the community;
- endeavour to initiate partnerships (and joint ventures) between the marginalized segments of the population and the rest of the community. (Brodhead 1994, 3)

In the original design and development years of the Weavers Cooperative, all of these characteristics were considered, anticipated, and launched. The project was primarily designed to create employment and to be a catalyst for economic activity. In this way, social benefits would accrue to the villagers. However, as the description of the Cooperative in the earlier chapters indicates, and as I will examine further in this chapter, the Cooperative has not actually fulfilled these expectations. The Cooperative still meets much of what is defined as CED according to the above objectives, but it has not been able to generate the community-level impact in the way described in the original project proposal.

But despite the apparent weaknesses or disappointments in the project, I think the Weavers Cooperative has achieved a great deal and can contribute to other CED ventures in Africa and elsewhere. The workers have demonstrated perseverance and patience, as they maintained production while bringing up their children, participating in village obligations, and generally improving their quality of life. The current workers have sustained themselves in a process of rapid economic and social change while other workers and supporters have come and gone.

The Cooperative itself has endured many difficulties and still suffers a serious dependency on foreign assistance. I will examine some of these difficulties and other elements of what makes Oodi Weavers the CED venture that it is. I will draw from its experience some of the lessons that can be useful for other similar ventures.

I expect that others will find many more lessons in the actual description of the Cooperative and in the testimonies that are quoted throughout the book. This is not an instructional manual, however; it seeks to expose and analyse features of CED so that others can implement them according to their local conditions, needs, and cultural resources. And this section is not an evaluation of the weavers; it does not judge what the workers are doing to improve themselves, though they have been involved in discussions that have led to the writing of the book.

Structural Elements

A starting point for exposing what the Oodi Weavers project can teach us is the basic framework of the venture, the structural features needed for a successful CED. In effect, the structural features are like the vertical warp of a tapestry, its skeleton that gives the CED venture its organizational and operational form. The three structural requirements that exist for most CED ventures or industrial cooperatives are development capital, knowledgeable workers, and market position. In different forms and to different degrees these three features will be in demand for each CED venture. They will demonstrate different characteristics according to each situation, but each has to be addressed effectively for the CED venture to thrive.

Development Capital

Many people who want to start CED activities or a specific CED venture usually think that the most difficult requirement is getting the money to start. And indeed, for many ventures, getting the initial funds to buy equipment, locate the facility, or pay the initial wages and operating costs is the major first step.

If a commercial loan is required, then the people behind the venture have major hurdles to leap, as most banks and other lending institutions lack a basic understanding of the CED approach and are rarely willing to take the risks inherent in these ventures. First, it is difficult for mainstream lending institutions to deal with CED projects or activities that by their nature lack material assets. The people who get involved in CED activities do not have a lot of property, money, or other physical assets to use for loan collateral security.

Second, these financial institutions find it difficult to know who can be held accountable in CED ventures. By their nature and objectives, CED organizations are democratic and decentralized, with obtuse lines of responsibility and accountability. Without a common appreciation of how economic and social goals can be integrated into an enterprise, banks and CED groups are often unable to bridge their different requirements to reach a common financial arrangement. Where representatives of these two camps have understood each other's needs or have created shared goals, the loan requirements have been fairly easily met.

If a grant can be obtained from a government agency or non-governmental organization, then a venture has a small advantage in that the financial cost of this asset can be reduced. While the organizations interested in funding CED are few, funds are available through cooperative banks, peer lending facilities, union-sponsored funds, charitable foundations, and, in some cases, community contributions and fundraising. But getting a grant often means adapting CED goals and methods to donor expectations, which can distort a project's direction and potential, thus adding other costs to its overall development. Donors, particularly government donors, tend to want to monitor and define how their money will be used, which implies some intervention in the operations of a recipient venture. These donor requirements and the related interventions have led some CED practitioners to doubt the commercial and social advantage of grants over commercial loans.

Once people get started on a CED activity, however, they realize that getting the initial capital is not the main problem to starting a venture. They soon realize it is only the first step in a complex and never-ending tension with money (or more accurately, with the lack of money). There will be continuing needs for capital to upgrade equipment and skills, maintain infrastructure, develop and diversify products, research new process options, and meet monthly cash flow requirements. While money will become a constant requirement for the venture, what becomes significant in creating successful ventures is how and by whom money is handled and controlled.

Who Pays? Now and Later

After an extensive review of financing possibilities for industrial producers cooperatives (IPCs), Abell and Mahoney conclude that it is the cou-
pling of finance to management that is critical.

> If one is committed to the promotion of IPCs then it will be necessary to
> establish a strong sector with some overall co-ordination and strategy
> deriving from a promotion agency endowed with appropriate funds. This
> agency must in some way through prudential oversight guarantee appro-
> priate management advice to those IPCs which need it, along with the
> requisite external capital. (Abell and Mahoney 1988, 399)

An underlying critical issue, however, is who will pay for the continuing development or social costs of such projects. How will the constant demands of supporting the poor — the people in these projects
who do not have the economic or political resources to be independent
— be subsidized? Development or social costs refers to the human or
ideological aspects of an enterprise that add to the overall cost of production, above strictly commercial costs. For example, if illiterate, dis-
abled, or untrained people are employed, the labour costs and therefore
the cost of production will be higher than in commercial ventures
where workers come trained and able.

Because of the social benefits of employment, government agencies
and some NGOs will sometimes provide training, building construction, or technical resources that the CED venture cannot cover. For private industry or business, either the individual workers or the
government, through institutionalized training, will in effect subsidize
their human capital requirements. And for the small, family enterprise it
is the owner and his/her family that subsidize the operational and developmental costs of their small business.

Mainstream or market economists have tended to ignore or down-
play the latent subsidies that market economies depend on. The conventional thinking is that private business operates mostly independently with
little help from government or social institutions. Actually, business can
only survive where there are government policies that support trade and
commerce and where workers provide a multitude of tertiary supports,
including those as parents and consumers. Fortunately, the work of
economists like Marilyn Waring have documented effectively the way
women and children bear the hidden costs of maintaining commercial
enterprises and, therefore, the profits generated (Waring 1988). Yet the
myth remains for many government and bank officials that CED projects
require and receive subsidies whereas private sector ventures do not.

The capital used to start Oodi Weavers came mainly from NGOs in grant form, except for a small loan from the Botswana Development Corporation. The Goweniuses very cleverly arranged for their CUSO salaries to be paid in full at the beginning of their contract, and then they used these funds to build the factory buildings. They put themselves on the line and demonstrated a confidence in the workers, who had to immediately start producing an income and, therefore, a wage for the Goweniuses. This required a brief start-up period for the factory, which allowed the workers to get involved and to take over within a relatively short period — in other words, they avoided the tendency for large, over-capitalized ventures that especially government has tended to start (and had wanted in this case).

The NGOs involved, the Botswana Christian Council and CUSO, also took an innovative approach to funding the project with some risks, which demonstrated confidence in the project concept and in the workers. They were clearly cautious about supporting such a new venture and did so largely on the basis of the Goweniuses' reputation. As both organizations also realized, supporting a project of this nature required more than funding, and they contributed other expertise and organizational support long after the initial funding was approved.

Since then, the weavers have only taken out one "rescue loan" in 1993 from the Department of Cooperative Development. They have not had a massive debt and persistent debtors to deal with, which could have been a serious burden to bear through the years of difficulties. For instance, they did not have to deal with a large debtor that would have demanded payment and, therefore, denied funds for other essentials, such as raw materials or salaries. For the poor, a debt is more than a financial obligation, often becoming a deadening moral weight, which the weavers have been able to avoid.

Foreign Aid

For a large part of what they have needed for business management, infrastructure development, and expansion, the weavers have turned to foreign donors: the Swedes, Canadians, British, Americans, and Japanese. While we can say that the actual contribution of the donors has not been huge over a 20-year period, it has been significant in recent years. Without the Peace Corps and Japanese volunteers, it is likely that the Cooperative could not have survived the last five years. The Department of Cooperative Development and, therefore, the Government of Botswana, have also helped subsidize some of their social costs through management advice, financial scrutiny, and cooperative training. On the other hand, considering how influential the Cooperative has been in improving the lives of at least 50 families in the village, contributing to village improvements and inspiring national development, these subsidies have been rather minimal.

However, the weavers have paid, and are paying, for some of their social costs through lost or deferred wages. They have provided the training and integration of new members into the Cooperative and, therefore, absorbed the cost of underproduction while these new workers gained experience before they met production standards. The collective management process has its social advantages for the members, but the entire Cooperative membership has paid for this process through decreased production while members hold meetings or participate in the management committee. Although actual money has not been paid out for these non-financial requirements and benefits to the workers, they have nonetheless paid for them.

The weavers have kept their cost of financing the project relatively low and have minimized the ongoing disruption that outside financing can involve. This has meant fewer complications for the Cooperative in terms of complex decision making and financial management. The weavers have not had bankers, NGOs, or government officials interfering with the operations of the factory. Even with their good intentions these donors do not have the same commitment to the factory that the weavers have and, therefore, do not share in the same future of the Cooperative. This is definitely an important advantage: keeping the venture small, minimizing the number of actors to be considered, and avoiding the moral burden of debt have allowed the weavers to retain control of the project, keeping ownership and authority in their hands. The weavers may not have reached their full potential, but they can take some pride in the fact that what has been achieved has been largely due to their efforts.

Limited Funding

Limited financing has also meant limited development for the Cooperative, which may have long-term detrimental effects. Without infrastructure expansion, skill upgrading, product diversification, and integration of new members, the Cooperative risks not being sustainable and not keeping up with new demands. Organic deterioration is taking place. The buildings are crowded. Workers are aging and leaving the factory. Revenue is not able to provide a sufficient wage for the weavers and for attracting new workers. Low revenue has also retarded the weavers' capacity to contribute to village development, a major objective for the project. It is possible that without a significant effort to expand production and sales, which would probably require new capital, the weavers may not survive beyond the life span of the members who have been with the factory from the beginning. A gradual decline in capacity can be averted but clearly there will be a need for development financing of the Cooperative — financing the weavers do not have.

Obviously self-financing is preferable, where revenues (customers) subsidize the costs of production and development. However, where external funding is needed, occasionally or situationally, the important consideration for CED enterprise is to retain control over how the funds are used and repaid. It is critical that the Cooperative members not succumb to the diversionary demands of donors or lenders.

Knowledgeable Workers

The importance of knowledge in CED action sounds self-evident, as every venture is based on some knowledge of what and how to produce a particular good or service. Especially in the contemporary globalized economy, it appears increasingly obvious that the extent to which knowledge or understanding is cultivated within the workforce will determine the success of that venture. As Flo Frank writes, "Human resources are our most renewable and value-added resource. With appropriate training they will allow movement into a new era of organization and production processes that can compete in the global market place" (Frank 1994, 237).

What is not so obvious is the scope of knowledge that is needed to foster a CED, the nature of that knowledge, and how knowledge is developed within a group of workers. By knowledge, I am referring to the technical, organizational, and social understanding that is needed by CED participants to function effectively.

Technical, Organizational, and Social Knowledge

The distinction between how private and CED enterprises view training and knowledge requirements is vast. In effect, the former see training as a business or production cost, which should be parcelled, packaged, and projected onto workers according to the needs of the business and the marketplace. CED projects treat training as a human development resource that must be integrated over time into the evolution of an enterprise and according to the needs of the workers and their communities as well as the enterprise itself.

At the technical level, workers need to know what goes into production and how to maintain the quality of their output. For example, it is important to know how equipment functions so that maintenance and repair costs can be minimized. Without effectively shared information on what is needed for efficient production, any commercial venture will fail. Workers also need a level of literacy and workplace rapport to enable them to do the technical work of production. It is at the technical or production level that private business and CED enterprise share some common interests in training. Whether in a privately owned business or a socially driven enterprise, improved production knowledge and skills are necessary to add value to any product or service being sold. Ongoing worker training is required.

In a CED enterprise, however, workers must also develop the knowledge that goes beyond the purely technical, to include organizational understanding and skills. To play their ownership and management roles, workers need to learn about organizational management, workplace relations, and their position in the marketplace. Workers in a CED venture must and can learn how to function within a collective work environment, to make joint decisions, to understand the needs for policy and procedures, to understand all aspects of business (for management purposes), and to deal with a dozen other operational issues that help workers play a full role in their venture. This knowledge can then be applied or adapted to other situations or within their personal and community life. It is at this level that workers can be intellectually empowered as they situate themselves in a structure of authority or power.

Similarly, for CED ventures to effectively play a role in their community development, the workers need to understand the workings of their communities as economic, cultural, and political entities. Through this social knowledge, individual workers can play a formative and directive role in their communities as well as in their families' and own lives. The perspectives gained in a global or social understanding of themselves and their roles in economic and cultural development can also be instrumental in motivating workers and helping them sustain productive participation in their cooperative.

For CED ventures with the poor, social knowledge is also a powerful mechanism for building confidence in themselves and helping them acquire the courage to play a serious role in managing their work and personal lives. Learning and training are not mere add-ons to a CED project, but a central imperative for every individual involved, to be maintained over the life span of the venture.

Continued Training

Technical and organizational training for Oodi Weavers was an established and major part of the venture from the beginning, and many of the workers still refer to this training 20 years later. Weavers who were trained by Ulla Gowenius often referred to her instruction. They would also mention Peder's efforts to improve the quality of their weaving. And the attention to training did not end with the Goweniuses' departure in 1978 but was maintained through brief returns to Oodi between 1979 and 1983 to upgrade the technical and management skills of the workers. Peder and Ulla also introduced management and political training so the workers could understand some of the issues that affected their ownership of the factory and their participation in the development of their village and nation.

Since the Goweniuses left Oodi, technical training has been largely left to the weavers to do on their own. They have been responsible for their own on-site upgrading and preparation of the new weavers. In the mid-1980s two other Swedish weavers augmented the weavers' skills by focusing on new clothing products. And the Japanese volunteer who came in 1995 was brought in to help improve and maintain the quality of the woven products. But overall, the weavers have felt that they have the technical skills to produce their products and, therefore, do not need other expert training. For example, they now feel they are able to maintain quality control through day-to-day interaction and informal communication among themselves. As a result of this attitude, most of the weavers have continued to produce crafts rather than objects of art. They have not expanded their vision or artistic treatment of their work and they have not passed on their skills to others.

At an organizational and management level, training of the weavers has been left totally to that provided by the Department of Cooperative Development. There have been some Department courses given in Oodi and at their facilities near Gaborone. Some of these courses have focused on management issues and bookkeeping, but most have explained the requirements or rules of cooperative organization. As already noted, the Department officials have acknowledged the limitations of the training they have provided to the Cooperative members. The expatriates who have worked at the factory have also tried to informally educate some of the workers on aspects of management, but overall there has been very little concerted attention paid to marketing or business management training.

The third level of knowledge — at the global or developmental level — has not continued at all. Since the Goweniuses left Oodi, the politicization that Peder emphasized in the early years of the factory has stopped. The workers clearly do want to contribute to village life as individuals who see a moral role for the factory in the village, but they have not made any effort to expand their understanding of societal or developmental issues.

Overall, it is remarkable that the weavers are able to maintain production quality and the management of the factory with so little ongoing training. Because they have not had the confidence to reach out for more knowledge, and since their cooperative structure has prevented individuals from initiating more comprehensive learning, their training and education have plateaued. What this situation shows, though, is an innate ability of key individuals and a collective commitment of the membership that have allowed them to function for so long. Their rudimentary academic skills and personal talent have sustained the factory despite the lack of training and evolution of formal knowledge.

However, the effects of limited training are now being felt by the weavers and serious fault lines are emerging:

- The lack of membership confidence in the management committee is a partial result of limited membership management knowledge. This is creating some conflict over operational issues. Key policies and procedures of the factory, such as how wages are determined or what management does for the workers, are not understood. This lack of knowledge is exacerbating suspicions and other dysfunctional attitudes the workers have about each other. Individuals holding positions in the management structure also feel they do not have the skills to do their work and are becoming disillusioned.
- The weavers do very little marketing or product development and are, therefore, restricted to a local and limited clientele. They need to build their market research skills, business development knowledge, and promotional confidence.
- The weavers have not collaborated with Oodi and neighbouring villages for a number of years as a formal development partner. They are now in danger of losing their community support. In this regard, they need to know what to do and how to do it.

As long as the factory is not threatened by serious competition, the workers are satisfied with a minimal return on their labour, and if they get continued expatriate expertise, the Oodi Weavers will survive. However, without an active educational effort among all the workers, it is highly unlikely they will be able to share effectively the responsibilities of ownership or management, or to initiate the organizational and community development they want and need.

Fundamentally, the Cooperative ideals and practical future are in jeopardy if some effort to improve the overall knowledge of the workers is not continued. As Frank Adams and Gary Hansen note,

> The relationship between democratic management and learning is organic. Democratic management facilitates adult learning and personal growth because all members have the right to know about the business; more importantly, they have the responsibility to know how their company works and how it can work better. This is the only way that members of a democratically managed firm can make wise decisions about its operation. (Adams and Hansen 1996, 138)

While the cost of training and the availability of expertise are often obstacles, these are not barriers if the workers have the confidence and drive to invigorate their enterprise. For a group to maintain this ongoing development component they need a collective spirit of development, akin to a sense of entrepreneurial adventure.

Therefore, a firm foundation in technical, organizational, and social knowledge is necessary for CED, but the training in these areas must be constantly active, relevant, and integrated into the endeavour. Specific training for individual workers and general education for the membership must be a sustained part of the enterprise and, therefore, a regularly planned part of its functions. As Flo Frank writes, "Most CED practitioners recognize that there is no one model or approach for community-based human resource development. Successful strategies are tailor-made and combine a number of elements or components" (Frank 1994, 242).

Market Position

The commercial marketplace is the natural terrain of business. For CED groups, who are generally driven by social goals, the marketplace is largely foreign ground. However, to exist and to thrive, a CED enterprise must compete on this terrain, or in what some people coldly call the "real world." While CED groups must and do adapt to the rules and requirements of this terrain, it does not mean they have to act like conventional businesses and forgo their developmental ideals and social principles.

To survive commercially in the marketplace in a market economy, people involved in the venture must understand the network of commercial relations that will affect its production or provision of service and, therefore, lead to a sustained revenue. Whether in a privately owned business or a socially driven enterprise, it is important to know who the competition are, who the customers are, what is cost effective, what advantages one has over the competition, and how to maximize profits. As most businesses realize, they must understand the market-place and be aware of the changes as customer interests and competition shift or turn completely around.

It is also important to link social, political, and economic phenomena to determine what people will want and then what they will buy — which are often not the same thing. It then becomes important to know how to reach out to these customers, distinguish one's products or services from the competition's, meet government rules and regulations, and deal with a number of other issues that help sell a product or service. In short, thorough market analysis and planning are prerequisites for any commercial or cooperative enterprise to survive and to be sustainable. The market position of a CED venture then becomes its resource base, its source of energy.

Whether a CED project is producing goods or services, creating employment, training people for employment, or starting small businesses, the marketplace will significantly influence what is possible and what should be done. The members of a CED enterprise must know its products or services well and which consumer needs and wants it can meet profitably.

Members must also know where their CED enterprise is vulnerable and where it is strong because of its social objectives and community ties. In the 1980s and 1990s in North America, numerous income-generating projects were started in response to public concern about being more environmentally responsible. This concern, however, did not lead to consumer demand when people realized they would have to pay more for such products and services. Some CED ventures — for example, those producing arts and crafts — also assumed that public interest was the same as consumer demand, and these projects failed because they could not generate sufficient revenue to continue.

However, while the social objectives of CED ventures do add costs to the product or service being sold, they are not necessarily market liabilities. Some CED groups, such as those working in the area of recycling materials, have found their social and environmental goals provided a certain market advantage, as their consumers agreed with the goals involved and were willing to pay to achieve them. There are also recent examples of consumers demanding more social responsibility and accountability of business, which has provided a market profile and advantage for them (the experience of The Body Shop chain is evidence of this global interest in socially responsible commerce).

"Wait and See" Marketing

The weavers' approach to cultivating their market position is a very passive "wait and see" method. They do very little advertising, hardly any promotional outreach, and while there is a friendly welcome at the factory when customers come, there is no customer-service ethic that encourages consumer repeat buying. As long as a steady flow of expatriates comes to Oodi, it is likely sales will remain high. However, this flow is not secure, and people's likes, dislikes, and buying habits are important factors, which the weavers are only now comprehending.

There have been some efforts to diversify their products and to include other crafts in their Oodi showroom to attract consumers, but these have been small undertakings with limited returns. There has also been very little effort made to modify their products to appeal to new customers. To continue weaver Tidimalo Tlhagwane's quote from chapter 1, "We only did one thing, village life, village life, so that when tourists came they were not pleased and they just went away." So at times sales went down and so did the workers' pay. While there have been endeavours to promote the weavers at trade fairs and agricultural shows, there have been few other attempts to engage the crafts marketplace, to cultivate a profile, and to increase clientele.

Part of the reason there has not been more assertive marketing is that the factory has been able to maintain a growth in sales over the last two years. As the weavers see the situation, their production is keeping up to sales and they cannot increase production with the current number of workers and in the facilities they have. Only a couple of the weavers said they recognize the need to expand sales to increase wages to a fair level, fund improvements, and create the expansion that is needed for the future.

Also, marketing is not seen as a high priority because there is very little domestic competition. Another weaving project that started up in Lobatse (to the south) in the late 1980s collapsed, and a small weaving group in Francistown (in the north) is still in production but their tapestries are distinctly different from the Oodi Weavers' work and, therefore, are not seen as direct competition. Because there were and are very few crafts in Botswana that have such an artistic quality, the Oodi tapestries have basically cornered the market and enjoy a monopoly that many businesses and CED enterprises would envy. But as new products become available to meet a growing tourist inflow, it is likely this situation will change.

The lesson to be learned for other CED ventures is that a unique product with little competition does not guarantee an adequate or sustained clientele and revenue. There is no assurance that a product will remain popular and that customers will buy it. A market position is never static or secure, regardless of how much apparent interest there is in a product or service. The weavers learned this in the early 1990s when the quality of the weaves declined and sales dropped sharply. Therefore, it is still important to study and understand the marketplace within which an enterprise is functioning and to adopt measures to constantly bring customers back and attract new ones.

On the other hand, the weavers' experience also shows how a social objective for an enterprise can become a marketing advantage. The "developmental" profile of the Cooperative creates an appeal for expatriates in Botswana who are interested in the country's development. Tourists and others in Botswana are buying these products as much for the social scenes and reflections of African reality, which are unique, as for their aesthetic qualities.

The Workplace Culture

There are also basic relationships affecting a CED venture that should be anticipated and planned for if a venture is to succeed. In effect, these elements create the workplace culture that has to be nurtured to support the workers — as producers and as people. Continuing to use the tapestry metaphor, these relationships are the wool that is woven horizontally across the warp, to bind the tapestry together into a coherent and unique whole. These three factors that are the binding elements of effective CED ventures are shared values, leadership style, and management capacity. There are some universal instructions that can be gleaned from the Oodi experience.

Shared Values

It is essential that those who participate in a CED venture or activity share a basic set of values and ideals. The CED method involves a multiplicity of tasks and people that must work together to achieve a common set of goals. This is the case for any economic enterprise, private or collective. However, for CED ventures, cooperation is essential and must be encompassing and voluntary — not forced, coerced, or obligatory — to be sufficiently and practically binding. A common self-perception, based on shared values, allows cooperation among a group of workers.

Obviously, the individuals involved in an enterprise will not share all perceptions and values related to their workplace. But there must be a sufficient compatibility or similarity of interests to allow for cooperation and collaboration. It is important not to idealize cooperative groups and assume they are homogeneous and conflict free. Like communities and social groups anywhere, cooperatives involve people with different backgrounds and expectations. Interactions are laden with potential conflicts, misunderstandings, and contradictory expectations.

If there are significant age, gender, ethnic, or geographic differences in the group, then a common set of objectives or benefits is crucial. Something that is important to all of the individuals is needed to focus the voluntary cooperation. There can be a certain amount of individual interest in the venture — and individual benefit — but if a CED venture only has individual interests in common, there will not be a strong basis for meeting social objectives and resolving the inevitable difficulties that arise.

For any CED venture, it is important to pay attention to creating and maintaining cooperative or collaborative values, internally and externally. This net or web of support relations among workers, or among workers and others in their community of interest, becomes practically essential. Internally, workers must find ways of accomplishing numerous tasks and duties that cannot be paid for or that cannot be easily defined and planned. When the inevitable problems and difficulties arise, workers need the confidence and trust in each other to withstand the pressures that can divide a group.

In a major study of Indian, Senegalese, and Peruvian cooperatives, Abell and Mahoney found that a cooperative attitude, which they defined as solidarity, was a critical feature in the success of producer cooperatives. "One of the most striking results to come from our case studies was an almost perfect correspondence between the success of a cooperative and what one might term its high level of solidarity, and conversely between failure and low solidarity" (Abell and Mahoney 1988, 367).

Externally, workers need to establish strong working partnerships with other groups, like-minded agencies, and social groups where there are cultural or economic affinities. These partnerships and networks provide the numerous financial and technical resources, as well as help foster a supportive atmosphere of optimism that contributes to overall problem solving and innovation.

In the weavers' case there appears to be a fair amount of cooperation, or what they call "unity," within the factory. The weavers have
held the factory together despite many difficulties, and while there are
many disagreements among the weavers, they choose, on a daily basis,
to work together. Their cooperation is based on common interest and
ownership within an experience of collective tribal obligation. Workers
obviously collaborate because they materially benefit from the factory
and the wages they earn. However, they collaborate largely according to
a style they know from other ongoing cultural experience.

Traditional Cooperation

In Botswana there has been an established tradition of village cooperation, based on kinship obligation and tribal survival. Through *ipelegeng*,
people were expected to share in certain collective duties that contributed to the overall well-being of the clan or village. However, this
cooperation based on affiliation and obligation has been eroded by
modernization and government policy that has introduced payment and
choice to the implementation of many traditional activities. For example, through drought relief programmes, the government paid people
to do many of the duties they formerly had done voluntarily, thus introducing the expectation of payment for all such labour.

According to Molefi Mogapi, former assistant manager of the factory and now a businessman in Oodi, "Today if the road is destroyed
by water, the people will want the council to do something about it. In
the past the chief would bring people together, explain the problem,
and they would do something about it. Today the government has
made people believe that the government will do everything for them.
But they cannot! That is why the VDC is failing and cannot lead the
people — they are seen as part of the ruling party and they are politicizing the people in the direction of the ruling party. The present political
ideology in Botswana has liquidated the spirit of self-reliance. When a
kgotla meeting is called, the people don't come, because they feel they
have been promised and promised too much. The result, in terms of
infrastructure: Botswana is a developed country, though understanding
is still very low, partially because of their education and partially
because of this government policy."

It would appear that the underlying common values that bind
the weavers together are vague and assumed. They share a common
need for income and they value individual perseverance and labour.
Beyond their shared history and geography, they hold a respect for
collective work and obligation. The weavers do feel a common

ownership and unity but it is rarely discussed or consciously culti-vated.

Though there is a history and cultural conception of cooperation, the weavers are experiencing the decline of voluntary cooperation. As one weaver quietly commented to me in confidence, "There isn't any spirit of cooperation [among the workers]. If there was, we would lis-ten to the manager and also accept the stories she will give us to do."

Cooperation among workers within the factory, as a distinct fea-ture of operating the Cooperative, has been left unattended. Within the factory there is very little coherent effort to foster the common values needed for cooperation. The weavers are doing even less to cultivate supportive relations outside the factory. The last cooperation-building effort on the part of the workers was the construction of the drift in 1975 to enable people to cross a river near Oodi.

There is some collaboration with the Department of Cooperative Development but they do not relate formally or regularly to any other cooperatives in Botswana. They may sell tapestries through Botswanacraft, but they have not aligned themselves with any other craft-producing or marketing groups to promote themselves or to establish a mutually supportive network. However, in the weavers' defence, to form partnerships or networks would mean having other similar groups or cooperatives in Botswana to align with, and there are very few. And to play a formative role in fostering the cooperative movement would demand organizational and animation skills the weavers do not have.

Individual Participation

The weavers have not sought a formal role in village development or culture, as they rely on their individual participation in village duties to maintain relations. They do participate in *kgotla* functions as a factory group (for example, contributing gifts to the National Service youth who finish their placements in Oodi), but this is responsive and occa-sional, and more of a social contribution than a developmental one.

The result of this situation is a very fragile cooperation or unity internally, and isolation from the outside world. There is a growing sense that the factory only provides jobs and that individual weavers are basically on their own, not part of a significant whole. The women who have been at the factory since the 1970s feel more unity and some soli-darity, but this is not shared by the entire worker body. On the other hand, when there has been a threat of interference the workers have apparently responded with one voice and expressed some solidarity.

Worker cooperation is a major requirement for such enterprises and one that organically exists to some degree where there are common economic or social interests. However, cooperation must be constantly cultivated to provide the sustaining support needed by the workers. Cooperation cannot be expected to thrive where it is not acknowledged, encouraged, and facilitated. Without this attention it is likely that the binding forces of trust and confidence among the workers will decay.

As Humphrey and Schmilz write,

> That trust matters for economic development is now well established. It is also clear that trust is often missing. What is less clear is how it grows and how it can be made to grow. . . . The interlocking between enterprise and the new models of industrial organization requires more than minimal trust. And they are not just models, they exist in practice, not just in advanced countries but also in developing countries. The practice is messier than the models, but it shows how trust can be fostered. (Humphrey and Schmilz 1996, 1, 40)

Thus, cooperative relations cannot be treated as a given in a CED venture; they are prone to change and are as fragile as democracy itself. For a group to collaborate effectively they must learn appropriate techniques of cooperation (for decision making, evaluation, or planning, for example), get to know each other as people, and constantly cultivate the organizational and interpersonal communication that feeds their common values. Effective cooperation also needs a confident outward-looking attitude and a commitment to collective problem solving. These factors are related to a group's self-image and level of understanding of its position in society, all of which emphasize the link between cooperation, leadership, and educational dimensions of effective CED.

Leadership Style

In CED activities, leadership is essential for both pragmatic and psychological reasons. Leadership — the ability to define and direct action, to articulate and inspire motivation towards particular goals — is needed for day-to-day practical purposes as well as for instilling the idealism or moral energy needed for sustained cooperative action. In privately owned business, the leadership process is relatively clear since the goal is maximum income or profit, and the daily direction comes from those who own the business and, therefore, have the most to gain from its success. In CED ventures the goals are often more abstract, strategies are complex, and the benefits and beneficiaries are more nebulously defined, requiring leadership with a different consciousness.

Leadership is generally perceived as a characteristic or role of individuals in a situation. Often we turn to the charismatic or more vocal people in a group, usually the men, and see them as the leaders. The daily tasks of defining what has to be done, when, by whom, and how usually fall to individuals in a productive enterprise. Certain individuals are able to articulate a vision for a group that helps focus attention and activity, or can personify ideals and goals which are often difficult to define.

However, collective leadership, which CED ventures tend to choose, can also provide these functions if organized, structured, and accepted within a group. In theory, collective leadership has the advantage of including more people in a process and building on such things as collective knowledge, energy, and resources. While collective sanction, in the form of public opinion or community positions, can be identified loosely, collective leadership is more abstract or situational and needs agreed-upon supports and definitions.

With collective leadership, such aspects as organizational purpose and vision become important, and formalized decision making is essential. A clear vision gives members of a group direction and a means of attracting support. Goals and objectives are important for planning and monitoring, and mission statements are useful for guiding decision making. A vision is also a useful device for motivating and encouraging membership since it provides the ideals beyond the day-to-day requirements of a venture or project that people often need and appreciate.

Though the Oodi Weavers project was formulated on the basis of clear and specific social ideals and objectives of a development vision, these have become largely taken for granted or lost over the years. New members are told about the social objectives but there is little emphasis on the importance of implementing them. The collapse of the Sethunya development fund, for example, has been regretted but there has been no collective effort to revive the fund and its role as an umbilical link between factory and village. Thus, over the years the purpose and goal of the factory have become more centred on providing jobs and wages, rather than development support to individuals and the community. The development vision of Oodi Weavers has virtually faded from view.

Organizational structure is similarly important for collective leadership so that everyone involved knows who is responsible for what tasks and how they all can and should interact. When leadership relies on an individual, more ambiguity in organizational process can be tolerated, because it is the individual who will carry the responsibility and authority to maintain the productive process.

Organizational Structure

The organizational structure — the way decisions are made, responsibilities defined, policies developed, and benefits shared — has similarly lost its initial direction and legitimacy for the weavers. For example, the initial management structure, where authority and accountability were to be jointly held among all members of the Cooperative, has been replaced by a virtual elite hierarchy that is increasingly inefficient and not respected. Similarly, ownership is not clearly defined and structured, so that members of the Cooperative only have vague perceptions and monthly deductions as evidence of ownership.

The barriers to an effective individual or collective leadership process emerging from within the Oodi Weavers may be found as much in Batswana culture as within the Weavers Cooperative experience. The way power is shared in a society, particularly between men and women, is a significant factor that will influence how individuals or groups exercise leadership in the workplace. In Botswana, women have traditionally had a silent and hidden role to play in community decision making. They were often denied a direct role in formal *kgotla* meetings and subjected to a subservient role in the home. Today women are sharing power more openly, taking a stronger position in the direction of their lives and the future of their nation. For the weavers, these changing relations of power have meant more freedom in defining the direction of their lives, though it has also meant more conflict in their relations with men and, in some cases, with other women.

Poverty creates social reticence and cautions that lead to suspicion and criticism of others and oneself in the workplace or community. These psychosocial dynamics then interfere with a group's ability to make decisions or define a common vision with confidence. A number of the weavers expressed the need for an externally hired manager, someone with specific authority to supervise and direct work. Calling for someone to manage according to familiar hierarchical ways is thus an expression of both analytic need and a lack of confidence in their own abilities to lead.

The result of these complex cultural dynamics in the weavers' workplace is that very little leadership is exercised, or is possible. No one person has emerged to encourage or offer the membership this kind of direction. While individuals have tried and, in some cases, taken the lead on issues, no one has been able to provide the articulate vision to mobilize the membership in a significant way over time. The only individual who had the group's support to play a leadership role was the Peace Corps volunteer Joan Hoff, who is White, mature, and who would leave after two years.

A collective leadership has not emerged; instead, there seems to be a reliance on the lowest common denominator defining a minimal collective position. As one weaver said, "We should all be the same, no one should be higher than the rest!" Issues like defining a wage formula become persistent problems that not only create confusion and disillusionment but also confirm perceptions of membership incompetence.

A lesson that can be applied to other CED ventures is that a form of leadership that all members agree to and have confidence in must be structured into a collective from its beginning. Without this leadership process, without the ability to lead a group through difficult decisions and to motivate constant collective contributions, the enterprise will continually flounder. The group will be vulnerable to outside pressures and forces and will tend to settle for the least the group can do, rather than achieving its potential. While education of the membership, regular communication within the workplace, and effective democratic procedures are all necessary for leadership, other efforts must also be present to build trust, confidence, and motivation among the workers.

Management Capacity

Management is often seen as being key individuals who hold authoritative positions in a company or workplace and essentially dictate to the others what should be done, when, and how. Management, in any organized setting, is conventionally perceived as the exercise of knowledge and power. However, the essence of effective management is a practical ability to create an environment that encourages and allows all workers to contribute their best efforts towards a common goal.

There are two levels of management at work in a CED enterprise. On a day-to-day basis there is a need for "operational" or "technical" management, where production decisions are made quickly and efficiently so that a group's product, services, or objectives can be delivered. Management must coordinate and monitor, supervise and problem solve, and deal directly and immediately with internal issues.

At another level there is "organizational" management, which deals with long-term needs of the entire enterprise and of the membership — those needs that will sustain an organization's ability to produce or serve. Organizational management involves maintaining the basic structures to ensure personal support, investment in equipment or infrastructure, and partnerships and other relationships.

In CED ventures, management is a conceptually complex arrangement of different people doing different tasks but sharing responsibility and, often, accountability. Cooperative regulations set out some standard management procedures, but even these are fragile in situations where the people managing are essentially the people being managed. In addition, people involved in CED projects may have had negative experiences with management or no experience at all, which complicates how they will view and address management responsibilities.

Within a CED enterprise, management is a forum for technical, political, and social dynamics. Management must constantly decide how to use organizational resources (financial, technical, and human) to their maximum advantage and benefit for all involved, not just for a few owners. As the authors of *Cooperative and Community Development: Economics in Social Perspective* write,

> Cooperative and community development require a [management] style that draws in all stakeholders and gives them voice, not a structure that imposes a single vision from above. Cooperatives require a relational style of management that recognizes diversity as a source of strength, not a forced or confrontational style that sees only one objective at a time. (Fairbairn et al. 1991, 84)

Education and Communication

To implement effective collective management requires a number of factors not normally considered part of the management structure of an enterprise. For example, collective management — worker management — requires an educated and informed membership. Fairbairn et al. note, "Education is likely the key issue here — adult education and organizing in cooperatives and in the community. The structures and the leadership can both be improved, but more important than any structure is the kind of community activism, ideas and energy that must feed into such structures" (Fairbairn et al. 1991, 84). Considering the low or non-existing management skills within the membership of CED ventures, there will be a demand for skill and knowledge development that is specifically management-oriented for workers who hold the key positions in the management structure.

Communication becomes an important functional and psychological element of the management structure and process, and a binding feature that affects all other elements of CED management: marketing, fundraising, training, human relations, and production. Regular communication is the only way to keep information flowing to workers so they can function effectively within the workplace as both owners and workers. And though communication cannot solve all the differences and problems that surface in CED ventures, it is an essential element for solutions to emerge, as resolutions can only be understood and implemented if there is an effective interaction among all the members. Communication that works well helps build confidence and trust among the workers.

Currently, there is only an informal information flow among the Oodi Weavers, with very little organized and regular communication. On the shop floor there is a constant exchange of views and information, and since many of the workers live near each other they share information outside the workplace as well. However, formal communication is seriously lacking. For instance, there are no scheduled worker meetings or management committee meetings; they are called only when there is a problem or an issue to deal with. One criticism stated by a number of weavers was that management was not interacting with the producers, thus not communicating; instead they are "just staying in the office, looking at the books." Misinformation is likely to emerge when communication is so informal.

Management Responsibilities

For the weavers, management has largely become the responsibility of two people (the manager and the bookkeeper), whereas the project was designed so that all workers could contribute to the management of the Cooperative. The election and rotation of management representatives were to ensure that all weavers learned some management skills and that they could more confidently understand and appreciate the work of those elected to manage, and support them in their central work. However, most of the workers feel they are incapable of holding management positions and, from a lack of alternatives, have continued to re-elect the same weavers to management positions.

After nearly 20 years of this management experience, the weavers have lost confidence in their overall management and, largely, in their ability to change it. Day-to-day management has narrowed to the functions of maintaining records, ordering materials, and holding management committee meetings. There is little proactive treatment of personnel issues, marketing, infrastructure expansion, or equipment maintenance. At an organizational level, there is very little attention being paid to worker replacement and training, to community and government relations, and to cultivating other opportunities to ensure the growth and survival of the Cooperative. In other words, neither the operational nor the organizational management are working well.

One of the reasons for this situation is that operational and organizational management is handled by one body on an ad hoc basis according to situational demands and to the motivation of the manager or the chairperson of the management committee. Partially because of Cooperative regulations, and partly because of the limited knowledge of alternatives, the weavers have one governing body — the management committee — that is responsible for both operational and organizational matters.

Since the Board of Directors was dissolved in 1981, no defined body has been solely responsible for long-term organizational and developmental issues of the Cooperative. As well, because of the immediacy of operational issues and the familiarity of the management committee members with production needs, they have tended to focus on the operational level of management. So problems that arise among the workers are more difficult to resolve because of the confusion of roles and authority.

Management for Other CEDs

For other CED enterprises, the weavers' management experience offers a number of lessons. First, effective collective management is based on extensive and ongoing education for those in management positions as well as for the membership as a whole. Education is an essential resource to enable workers to know what to do and how it should be done. Knowledge builds the collective authority and confidence to permit those in management positions to enforce decisions and ensure quality performance.

A second lesson is the importance of simplicity and clarity in management. For example, management should immediately publicize its decisions and make clear how and why it made them. A management structure does not have to be complicated and burdened with procedures. However, it must be accepted and understood by all members of the enterprise if it is to be effective.

Third, the structure of organizational decision making, divided according to production or policy functions, for example, is critically important to a democratically run enterprise. Management functions that can be centred on individuals in private or public enterprises must be built into the organizational structure and procedures for CED enterprises.

What is unique to the CED enterprise or workers cooperative is that workers must play different and in some ways contradictory roles in the management of their enterprise. They must manage collectively (as owners they share accountability) and yet there is a lot they must do individually (on the basis of their own discipline and quality of work). They must take control, with full responsibility and accountability, and yet they must give up control to colleagues who are designated to carry out specific management duties.

Specific Oodi Features

For the Weavers Cooperative there are other formative issues to deal with that are specific to their situation. It is useful for us to examine how they have dealt with issues of ownership, wages, the management committee, and village development. While these are specific issues that the workers have identified and that arise regularly for them, they are also issues that arise in other CED ventures. Each of these issues — ownership, wages, committee management, and village development — was introduced in chapter 4, and I will now reflect on their significance in later years.

Ownership

Before the Goweniuses left Botswana, the issue of ownership was a major concern for the workers. Very few of them believed that the Swedish couple would leave when they said they would and that the factory would then be owned by the workers. Many of the workers acknowledged that it was intended that they would take over the factory, but few were confident this would happen or understood what it actually would mean in practice.

There was no precedent in Botswana for such a development and none of the workers had ever heard of such a handing over of a company in South Africa. Considering what the Batswana knew of White people, just the concept of giving such a resource to the people must have sounded totally illogical. As Mmatsela Dintwe, one of the original weavers said, "We told [Peder] that we don't agree. Seeing is believing. He said that those who stay here when he leaves will be the owners of this factory. We have never seen such a thing in Botswana that the workers could be given an industry like this one, but we will see when he goes."

The workers agreed to monthly deductions from their wages to purchase shares in the Cooperative, and this concretized their ownership. When questioned about their ownership of the factory 20 years later, many of the workers referred to these deductions and their shares as proof of ownership.

Some of the senior weavers, who knew the history of the factory and how ownership was conceived initially, referred to their ownership in other personal and conceptual terms. They repeatedly noted that they are solely responsible for the factory and that it is theirs and for their children. Some said it was this sense of ownership that drove them to maintain the factory in the profitless years from 1989 to 1994.

However, some of the weavers expressed doubts about the ownership of the factory — not outright denial, but scepticism that they were in full control of the factory, which they considered a measure of their ownership. For example, some said they felt there was unequal control of the factory by the workers since they were powerless to initiate policies and make decisions. Some said they felt under the control of the two management people, who seemed to be the actual owners of the firm. One person noted that she thought the Department of Cooperative Development was the ultimate owner as Department officials could close them down if the factory could not function or if the accounts were not done properly.

A couple of the weavers noted the complexities associated with ownership and, therefore, the problems they have to deal with that otherwise would not arise. Tidimalo Tlhagwane reported on a common concern, that individuals would abuse cooperative ideals for their own advantage. "We understand the firm is ours and we realize that if something happens to the firm it will be bad for us, but we say we are just equal and we can do what we like, for there is no one who can retrench [fire] us, no one who can do anything about us, we are all equal." And Selebaleng Ndaba related ownership to motivation and noted that the workers did not share equal motivation, or at least did not seem to treat their factory with equal attention. Others recognized that their limited understanding and knowledge is a barrier to full appreciation of what ownership involves.

A Sense of Control

Ownership means different things to different workers. Because there has not been a continuing educational or cultural effort to forge a common understanding of ownership and because there is an unequal division of responsibility for ownership duties, the workers have developed their own varied perspectives. Other than comments made by a couple of the senior weavers, we did not hear anyone talk in collective terms about their ownership. There did not seem to be a strong sense of collective responsibility for the factory and, in fact, some of the senior weavers lamented this deficiency.

As vague and divergent as the perceptions of ownership are, it is clear that the weavers do have a sense of their control over the firm and an accompanying sense of responsibility and accountability for it. They spend extensive time in meetings, and that time is not paid. They tolerate relatively low wages for prolonged periods, which demonstrates a commitment beyond mere employment, as does the low turnover of members. And clearly, if they did not own the factory, the members who worked without pay during the near-collapse period in 1994 would not have done so, and its collapse would have been ensured.

It appears that if more organizational attention was paid to cultivating an appreciation and a spirit of collective ownership, there would be a stronger commitment to the factory's survival and, therefore, a more collaborative effort when dealing with the issues facing the weavers. Because the management committee is focused on operational issues, the Cooperative members do not have a clearly identified forum for the regular treatment of organizational issues. If they had, they could cultivate a stronger appreciation of what ownership means and implies.

If there was more effort put into describing the share ownership of the factory to the members, and to regularly updating them on the status of shares, their ownership might appear less hypothetical. While ownership of the factory or enterprise may be abstract, ownership of the shares is more tangible as these are actually bought by the workers. Therefore, constant attention should be paid to the shares as a link to factory ownership and related member responsibilities.

Currently, for most of the weavers, ownership is a binding feature, a unifying component, but one that seems fragile, underutilized, and occasionally abused by individuals. Without focused attention, it will likely remain a weak binding feature or a declining one, dependent on senior weavers to occasionally articulate a commitment to the factory and, thus, keep the spirit of ownership alive. And without renewal of what ownership is and means for all the members of the Cooperative, there is little possibility that the overall commitment and contribution to the Cooperative will improve.

Wages

The workers' concern for adequate and fair payment for their labour has been a difficult and divisive issue since the project started. There have been numerous wage formulas and constant incremental changes over the years, and yet no complete agreement on any of these has existed for long. In early 1997, the wage formula was extremely complex to calculate and understand, and for some of the workers the existing system was breaking down.

While I was at the Cooperative, a major discussion took place dealing with the issue of wages. It reflected the complexity of thinking that is going into managing the Cooperative and how the workers are dealing with these issues. The management committee received a letter from 11 workers who claimed the wage system was unfair since it allowed some workers to get paid more while the main producers — that is, the tapestry weavers — were not paid enough. They felt that all workers should receive the same base wage. The committee had agreed to a small increase in wages the previous month but it had not been implemented. They were now going to address a former complaint that overall wages were generally too low. For about two hours the committee discussed both the increase and the complaint about unfairness. They could not resolve what should be done, so spontaneously they took the issue to a full gathering of the weavers.

The discussion that followed for the next two hours was dynamic, at times aggressive and at times humorous. A variety of views were offered, though only about a third of the weavers spoke up. The issues and different viewpoints were defended, and much of the discussion that ensued involved members restating what they thought should be done. A compromise agreement was suggested whereby wages would be increased for all of the weavers, but there would be small reductions for some of the workers who were receiving a higher base wage before. However, no vote was taken to confirm who and how many workers supported the agreement. Within a few days it was evident that no one was comfortable with the apparent decision that had been made at the meeting, and their complaints and informal discussions continued. The management committee came up with other recommended changes that did not satisfy everyone, so at the end of a week of eclectic debate there was only more confusion and disagreement.

Interrelated Issues

This episode exposes how the workers are dealing with multi-level and interrelated issues that frequently arise for them. They are practically dealing with a heterogeneous mixture of questions that have a direct impact on their work and their lives. During the wage discussion, I observed the following:

- The workers were in effect making policy through practice. The wage policy, which in other employment situations would be set by a board of directors, for example, was being defined by the worker-owners as they grappled with immediate income concerns. While it could be considered a conflict of interest, they were making decisions about themselves, for themselves, and by themselves because of the organizational structure.

- There was an evident lack of knowledge, or at least an imbalance of understanding, among the weavers. Frequently throughout the discussion, individual workers asked questions about the current wage and bonus formula, which indicated that they did not really understand how the system worked. There was very little background information presented to the workers on what their recommendations would cost or whether the Cooperative could even afford the increases being suggested.

- The workers were dealing with a workplace situation where some people were evaluated and measured for productivity but others were not. The tapestry and loom weavers, whose daily and monthly productivity can be concretely measured in how much they weave, were in effect evaluated constantly, and had their income determined by their effort (through the production scale and sales bonuses). On the other hand, the finishers and office workers (the manager and the bookkeeper) were never evaluated, and their income was fixed regardless of their efforts.

- There was a perceived social divide between the management and the producers, and between older members of the Cooperative and the younger. Clearly there were different opinions offered from the older and younger groups on the matter of equal base pay, with the former against it and the latter for it. A couple of the younger weavers said that they felt as if they were under "bosses."

- There was very little leadership or facilitation displayed for decision making. No one took on the role of helping the group to sort through the issue, clarify information, explain what people meant, propose options, and guide the group towards a feasible agreement. However, in the end there appeared to be some agreement, so the process, as confused as it appeared to an outsider, could be said to have worked.

Compare this incident to a conventional employment situation where workers have virtually no influence over their wages, which are arbitrarily set by the managers or owners; or compare it to a unionized workplace where wages are formally negotiated and rigidly applied.

The wage formula issue points out the complex interaction of contingent factors involved in implementing one operational issue in a democratically managed, socially conscious enterprise. Also, any operational formula will fail to meet member needs unless there is an organizational structure with the authority to make decisions, an educated membership that understands and accepts the decisions, and a workplace culture that is built on trust and discipline.

Management Committee Effectiveness

Another lingering and serious issue for the weavers is the effectiveness of the management committee, the formal body responsible for managing all the functions of Oodi Weavers. In interviews with the weavers there was a constant stream of complaints about the MC — more criticism than on any other single issue or feature of the Cooperative.

The workers not on the MC felt they were excluded from management and could do nothing about who was on the committee or what they do. Many weavers said they were generally dissatisfied with the performance of the MC, but this may have been more an expression of powerlessness than an informed evaluation and assessment of performance. But many said they were unprepared to play a role in the organizational structure of the Cooperative. While many were on village committees and knew how to play a role in traditional village consultations, they said they had not had training specifically directed at their responsibilities as owners and workers in the same productive enterprise. They, therefore, felt that they operated with insufficient knowledge, a constant ambiguity about their role in the decision making process of the organization, and a sense that they could not have an impact in any case because of their limited formal education.

Because the MC and the manager were identifiable they were singled out for criticism. As pointed out earlier, there were serious management deficiencies at the Cooperative, both in the structure of the organization and in the skill base of the membership. But these deficiencies were not as evident to the workers as they were to the people who were trying to deal with these issues that affect the Cooperative directly. The criticism of the committee was also a reflection of the lack of control some of the workers feel over their work; when a researcher was available to listen, it was understandable that they would express themselves in a critical way.

Members of the MC also felt they were powerless to reach and implement decisions. They spoke a great deal about being ignored and often criticized. They said they would make decisions but the workers would not implement them, for example. From their viewpoint, it is understandable that they were frustrated and feeling besieged. They were dealing with a rather complicated situation, burdened by an ambiguous organizational structure, virtually without support and without appropriate training for the tasks and responsibilities involved. The manager and the bookkeeper did not have assistants or seconds, had no supportive evaluation to help them improve their performance, and were also subject to incessant challenges from the membership, making them unable to offer serious assistance to the committee members.

The people who perform management functions in such enterprises tend to attract criticism, particularly if there are operational problems and underlying imbalances in the sharing of power, since they are the most visible link between problem, cause, and effect. They are the easiest people to blame if something goes wrong and especially if an adequate explanation for the problem is unavailable. If criticisms persist, then competent workers will refuse to participate and a tendency to involve the weaker workers will contribute further to a sense of management inadequacies.

As long as the MC continues to function as it has, and particularly if it remains responsible for both operational and organizational issues, the members will be under fire from the general membership. It is hard to imagine how the committee could initiate even the simplest of operational decisions when they lack the understanding, support, and confidence of the full membership. Or if they try to initiate changes to the structure of the Cooperative in order to improve the management of the factory, they will have to convince the membership of their genuine intent as well as the merits of the changes. Therefore, to improve the performance of the MC it will be necessary to improve the overall knowledge and understanding of the membership so they can elect and support a management committee they entrust to represent them.

To establish a competent and credible management committee requires a complex system of structural and educational supports. Training in management skills for these individuals or hiring a manager alone will not create effective management. An organizational authority (such as a board of directors) is needed, one that clearly defines the duties for the MC, gives them authority, and then backs them with a disciplined and committed workforce. Isolated, single solutions will not solve the problems faced by a management body in any CED enterprise.

Village Development

The well-articulated intention to foster economic development in the villages of Oodi, Modipane, and Matebele was part of the original Oodi Weavers project plan, and it was a goal many of them were proud of. According to the expatriates who gave birth to the project, this was to be the main reason for the entire venture. Though it was not mentioned spontaneously in interviews, many of the weavers expressed a strong interest in being part of the development in their home villages.

However, this objective has clearly not evolved to the extent initially expected for the weavers project or to the extent that some of the weavers would like. The Cooperative has not stimulated the additional jobs Gowenius defined in the project proposal. The project has not provoked the type of community development Dal Brodhead points to as part of effective CED, that which improves the "local capacity to plan, design, control, manage and evaluate initiatives aimed at revitalizing the community," and which incorporates "a comprehensive development approach which aims at linking economic, social, cultural, environmental and other sectors of the community" (Brodhead 1994, 3).

At a basic level there have been identifiable economic benefits and spin-offs for the villages. The weavers collectively earn about P10,000 to P12,000 monthly. While some of this revenue will be spent outside the villages, a great deal has been spent on home and agricultural improvements that employ local labour. Also, from the number of shops that now operate in the village, it would appear that some of the revenue from the factory is being spent for locally produced food products. No study has been done, however, to determine how much revenue from the factory stays in the village.

It is difficult to determine the overall economic impact the factory has had on the village because of the other economic changes that have taken place, particularly in Oodi, because of its proximity to Gaborone. As described in chapter 3, the village has grown significantly and is now a thriving suburban community, partially serving the housing needs of people working in the capital. Residents in Modipane and Matebele see the lack of similar growth in their villages but also feel that with water and electricity coming they will see significant incremental development.

The Sethunya Development Fund was intended to be a formative vehicle for extending the benefits of the Oodi Weavers project into the village and, thus, fostering social development for others. The fund got off to a good start but by about 1986 started to lose momentum and purpose, and within a couple of years had virtually faded from everyone's memory.

The fund's decline was partially caused by the Cooperative's inability to continue creating enough profit to deduct 25 per cent for village development. Many of the loans given out were not repaid. Cooperative rules were interpreted extremely literally so that the workers assumed they could not legally have a village fund. There also seemed to be a loss of interest on the part of the weavers, so that today few of them know what happened to the fund or why.

The impact that individual weavers are having on village life and development is striking, however. A number of the villagers I spoke with noted the improved houses of the weavers and said this physical improvement was important for village spirit and pride. In the 1977 study, many of the villagers attributed the availability of water in the village, a major development, to the presence of the factory. Weavers and former weavers have also become important members of many of the village committees, such as the Village Development Committee, the Parent Teachers Association, and the Oodima Junior Community Secondary School Board of Directors. Village leaders recognized the contributions to the village by individual weavers and said they could be counted on to participate in village obligations and events.

According to a Motswana researcher who was completing her Ph.D. thesis on community participation, and who met a number of the weavers in 1989,

> The community participation spirit expressed here [among the weavers] is definitely different from the one we saw in the community development programmes. Here, there is spontaneity and willingness. Individuals, having been lifted out of the misery of poverty and basic needs are now able to spread their wings from individuality to communal efforts. There is evidence of self determination to forge ahead brought out by the self discovery of one's growth potential. . . . It is the most outstanding example that confirms our assumptions that as people get liberated from the basic needs poverty trap and rise higher on the ladder of needs, they feel more secure and their horizon widens to see other problems around them and to determine to alter those. Because their capacity to do so has been increased, the likelihood of such people carrying out such endeavours is higher than those who are on the first level of need. (Mogome-Ntsatsi 1989, 341)

National Pride for the Oodi Weavers Project

Ironically, those people furthest from the factory, those with the least understanding of the factory's operative realities, still treat the Cooperative as a national developmental inspiration. Radio Botswana and the national magazine *Kutlwano* have often featured the weavers as a major success story, which is important to creating a supportive ethos for developmental initiatives. Government officials have paraded international guests through the factory to demonstrate what Batswana can do. But little of this has directly led to project replication, to parallel project creation, or to official support for the weavers.

However, is it fair to expect the weavers to promote broader developmental goals when they have to struggle so much to maintain a fragile economic venture, and particularly if no supportive network or national idealism exists to work with? It may not be just to expect a lone group of rural women to actively motivate other development initiatives under these conditions.

As the former assistant manager of the factory, Molefi Mogapi, said, "The political economy of this country is not helping [the weavers] to survive. Why? For example, take *ujamaa* [a strong sense of community or cooperation] in Tanzania, where the government is behind the people — that is totally different than [what is happening] here. The weavers are just a project here, not associated with the planning for the country, like in Tanzania. There was some support for the project in the *kgotla*, but the *kgotla* and the councillor perceived it as a project that benefited that group of workers only. They thought that problems at the weavers could and would be solved by the workers themselves. They did not relate the project to the village, only to the target group there."

The developmental impact of the weavers on the villages has, therefore, been incidental and sporadic, largely dependent on individual weavers rather than on directed collective intent. This experience indicates that it is still through the interplay of individuals that development change takes place. While organizational interventions may accelerate innovations, it remains the daily relations of individuals, through seeing what people do as well as hearing what they say, that will be the conduit for community development.

And circumstances change over time, which may mean development strategies should also change. When the Oodi Weavers project started it was never imagined that the country would grow so extensively and quickly on the basis of the vast diamond revenues, thus changing the character of the villages so much. While community development objectives may still be valid, an organization not only needs the capacity to implement them but the flexibility to adjust as situations change. Groups need ongoing planning and analytical skills to be able to adapt as their circumstances change. Community development, therefore, remains an ongoing interactive process determined by people's needs and capacities, not by organizational objectives and intentions alone.

Conclusions

The particular lessons we can identify for other community economic development ventures can be summarized:

- *Self-financing of a CED enterprise is preferable.* It is important to retain control of how developmental and operational funds are used and repaid. By keeping the cost of financing relatively low, the ongoing demands that outside financing involves can be minimized. However, limited financing also means limited development and sustainability, which has its own risks.
- *Relevant and ongoing training is necessary for a CED enterprise.* This technical, organizational, and social training must be constantly active and updated for an enterprise to thrive, as well as to merely survive. Workers also need confidence and drive, a "collective spirit of development," which can only partially be cultivated through education.
- *A unique product with minimal competition does not guarantee a sustained income.* While adequate revenue may be generated from products, those items will not necessarily remain popular. Therefore, it is important to understand the marketplace in order to maintain existing customers and to develop new internal and external markets.
- *Cooperation among a group is a major requirement for CED.* Like other training, cooperation must also be constantly cultivated. Common economic and social interests are the foundation on which the workers can begin learning techniques of cooperation.
- *Some form of strong leadership must be built into a CED enterprise in its early stages.* A capable collective leadership will build confidence and help a group to prosper. Leadership that fosters the trust, courage, and commitment to the cooperative will motivate workers to contribute to the democratic process.
- *Effective education is needed for those in management positions as well as for the rest of the membership.* It is key to provide all workers with the knowledge of collective management issues so that they are aware of the process and confident enough to enforce collective decisions.

- *Operational issues must be handled within a solid organizational structure.* Without adequate leadership mechanisms, formal membership relations, and a consciously maintained workplace culture, any decision, resolution of a problem, or new initiative will fail to meet collective needs.
- *Development strategies must change as circumstances change.* An organization must be flexible enough to adapt to different situations and to people's new requirements and positions. Community economic development, therefore, will remain an ongoing interactive process.

To extract broader lessons from the Oodi Weavers experience is more difficult, because a complex network of factors, all interacting obtusely, is likely responsible for what the weavers have achieved. Their ability to tolerate ambiguity, their artistic dexterity, opportune interventions of supporters, a solid organizational beginning, and a fairly buoyant national economy have played major roles in helping the weavers keep production going for the 20 years since the Goweniuses left. While it is impossible to measure the impact of any single factor, it is fairly certain that a juxtaposition of numerous planned and unplanned features is responsible for the weavers' survival despite setbacks, numerous internal frailties, and external deficiencies.

The experience of another workers cooperative in Botswana may put into perspective how an eclectic mix of cultural factors and structured supports has led to sustained production. The Thusano Silversmiths, a group of 12 Batswana youth that started their cooperative silversmith venture in 1983 (a venture that had virtually collapsed by 1989), shared many of the weavers' organizational experiences, but was distinctly different. In his concluding commentary on an analysis of the cooperative, Malcolm Harper wrote,

> It is obviously difficult to promote industrial employment of any kind in Botswana, with its traditional pastoralist society, but it was clearly a mistake to attempt to build a business which had no basis whatsoever in the potential members' existing skills or traditions. It is correct to try to add value to local resources such as silver and gems, but people are the most fundamental resource, and their skills and interests are a more important determinant of business success.
>
> From the beginning, the trainee members were treated as employees rather than independent business people. They were paid regular wages throughout their training period, and at no time does it appear that any thought was given to management, as opposed to the technical skills.
>
> The members had problems from the beginning because of their lack of financial management and marketing skills, but the official response

was to give them 22 pages of by-laws and intensive training in coopera-tive law and practice, rather than in the basic management which is needed for any business, whatever its legal form.

There was no leader in the group, and the only person who knew anything about keeping records was the woman who appears to have had no authority over the other members. The members followed the official rules by electing a five-member management committee, when there were only six members in the whole group. This is a typical example of how official rules can damage a vulnerable group. It would almost cer-tainly have been better for the Thusano Silversmiths if they had never officially registered as a cooperative at all. (Harper 1992, 74–75)

Some of the weavers' achievement was the result of wise organiza-tional preparation, such as the location of the factory in one central vil-lage and inclusion of workers from a broad familial cross-section of the three villages. The attention to quality production (a commercial pre-requisite) and village development goals was also important in keeping the workers focused and customers promoting the weavers' products. However, it would be misleading to imply that they implemented good business practice and that this is why they have achieved some success. Clearly they have not conducted the member education, management training, product promotion, community outreach, and a dozen other things that logically lead to successful cooperative production.

A primary broad lesson to take from the Oodi Weavers' experience is that there are no clear givens, no pure truths in CED, but rather suc-cessful CED action depends on cultivating an ongoing process that allows a number of factors to flourish. While there are some factors we generally know are effective in CED efforts — for example, the practi-cal value of worker participation in management — even these depend on situational conditions and may not be universally applicable.

In many ways, starting a CED enterprise is tantamount to launch-ing out on a journey more than engaging in a commercial venture, and there are numerous surprises, changes, adjustments, and failures to be expected. Like any adventure or journey, the route is rarely predictable, and often the more difficult and convoluted the route, the more mean-ingful is the resultant learning. The issues and elements raised in this chapter for CED enterprises are, therefore, only signposts or guidelines along a route, available for use or not, according to the circumstances and needs of each group.

CED process may be convoluted or elliptical, and rarely direct, but assuredly there will be numerous factors to consider simultaneously. It would appear that a main bond in this mix of factors affecting the Oodi experience is that commitment to a cause, with its related motivation and tenacity, is a key requirement for a sustained CED enterprise. Because a core group of women consider the factory to be theirs and have a responsibility and obligation to it, they possess a commitment that is critically important to the factory. They do have a motivation (albeit fragile) to sustain their project, a determination and dedication needed to maintained production through the bad times. Their sense of ownership provides the means to weather difficulties and to continue production despite minimal material benefit.

For the Oodi Weavers, ownership is not merely physical possession or legal control of property. Ownership is a living opportunity to exhibit a potential, to have some influence over their lives (though not complete control), and to be creative in ways otherwise denied. Ownership of the Cooperative represents something meaningful to be associated with, to be proud of, and to be identified by. Ownership provides a personal and collective reference point within a cultural and community context that is changing dramatically and quickly losing its familiarity and security.

It is unscientific but nonetheless a valid observation that if a group is focused on their project (issue, cause, ideal, etc.), if they are "determined and dedicated," as the primary school headmaster said, then they have an energizing foundation to build on. Determination, based on something as nebulous as a sense of ownership, may seem out of place in an analysis that is trying to identify tangible lessons for supporting practical CED, but this factor is a central contributing element in the weavers' achievements.

A related conclusion that can be drawn from the weavers' experience is that a people's culture provides the base knowledge and visions the workers need to function within their new working environment. While the roles, meanings, and values imbedded in their language and social behaviour are often ephemeral, these cultural factors have a concrete influence on their lives as workers in the Cooperative.

The weavers have created their own method of operations that are rooted in their community and cultural history — hymns that begin each work day, endless hours of discussion, meticulous record keeping that has little real management value, financial contributions to conventional (not developmental) village events. As the weavers have appropriated a visual art form to express their traditional storytelling, they have also appropriated the worker-cooperative form to express their capacity to manage and care for their new work environment. Their methods may be neither systematic nor commercially efficient but they work — to some extent! The weavers may not be performing to the standards expected by other people, but they have created a strong nucleus of interests, and they have a commitment to Oodi Weavers that has the capacity to maintain the Cooperative.

The workers — the women and the few men who have laboured at the factory for so many years — have demonstrated perseverance. They continue to produce beautiful woven products, operate their Cooperative, and weather near collapses. At the same time, they manage to bring up their families and contribute to the quality of life in their villages. They control their workplace far more than they could in any other form of employment available to them, and, therefore, they continue to benefit significantly. They are the success of the venture.

The Cooperative is a complicated and qualified achievement as an enterprise, but an achievement nonetheless within the context of their lives and their community life. Considering the little they have had to work with, the weavers have succeeded more than they have failed. Despite the apparent near collapse and weaknesses of the Oodi Weavers as a workers cooperative, it has accomplished and demonstrated a great deal. This is not to say that everything the weavers have done is right and that what they have done well should be replicated. This assessment of their achievements is only to emphasize the value of what they can teach others interested in workers cooperatives or CED enterprises. The follow-up, the application of what is learned to new conditions and other circumstances, is up to us.

Of course, the Cooperative is still operating and the members are still dealing with the issues discussed in this book. They will have new opportunities to meet their needs and to contribute to other cooperatives and village developments, in their own way and on their own terms. They may still fail as a producers cooperative; however, as one of the weavers, Selebaleng Ndaba, said to me, "I think by the year 2000, according to my wishes, we could still be operating. Even if you are at home with your husband and you are having a conflict, later on you get used to this kind of life and you continue fighting because there is no alternative, there is nothing we can do but to go on."

Epilogue

In May and June of 1997, meetings took place between the weavers and certain prominent villagers. Though there had been extensive informal contact between the weavers and the villagers, there had been very little formal rapport in the last decade and no official support offered when the weavers needed help.

Provoked by the research for this book, and initiated by the headman for Oodi, the first meeting took place. The headman invited ten selected important people from the village and the Oodi Weavers' management committee. This meeting was intended to be an opportunity for me to report on my research. It quickly became a much more important dialogue between these community leaders and the weavers. Because it was the first time some of the selected villagers had formally met with the weavers, they had many questions, such as what was produced at the Cooperative, how it operated, and what were the main problems experienced by the workers. The weavers provided a candid view of their internal activities and they readily noted some of their management and operational difficulties. While it was a somewhat cautious and exploratory conversation, the people involved were clearly willing to continue discussions on how the Cooperative and the village could work together.

Following this initial meeting, villagers and Cooperative members met to discuss what could be done specifically to help the Cooperative and to avoid another near collapse of the factory. There was a tour of the factory for some of the VIPs, and another meeting was held with all of the members of the Cooperative to discuss the problems the weavers were facing in keeping production going.

At the time, I thought this initiative indicated a turning point for the weavers. I saw it as a fragile but significant step as they grappled with their management difficulties and exercised their social and economic potential. I saw this set of meetings as a formal communication bridge between the workers and the community that could open up desperately needed organizational relations and allow the management changes needed.

A year later, virtually nothing had happened. The Cooperative members had not taken advantage of this offer of community support. There is no doubt that the people of Oodi could provide a great deal of help if the Cooperative members or manager could articulate what they need. There are business people, political leaders like the district councillor, and experienced long-time supporters like Sandy Grant who could muster the necessary assistance.

From one perspective, this lack of progress, this likely "opportunity lost" is another indicator of entrenched weaknesses in the Cooperative that are limiting its operations. The weavers' response to the village could reflect their management confusion, a lack of innovative leadership, and the lack of momentum in the cultural conditions that surround the workers, locally and nationally. It seems like a vicious circle: the weaknesses in the Cooperative management are preventing the Cooperative from taking advantage of offers of help that would correct the management weaknesses.

From another perspective, this situation exemplifies the complex nature of decision making within Oodi Weavers and the controls used in such democratically owned enterprises. This situation demonstrates the authority the weavers have over their firm, and, though debatable, their lack of response could be logical and necessary.

The weavers are exercising a power and control that is fundamental to their project and to development projects in general. There are times when this democratic control becomes dysfunctional (for example, on the issue of wages), but it is also possible to understand how this fragile exercise of control keeps the Cooperative small enough to be somewhat manageable for the weavers. More importantly, it is the workers themselves who are accountable to and responsible for themselves, and whether they do or do not take advantage of opportunities, it is they who will benefit or suffer. In a convoluted way, this situation demonstrates a particular success of the project in empowering the workers by cultivating a level of membership power that is an underlying objective of the Oodi Weavers project and all CED enterprises.

Empowering Participants

Empowerment is a very popular term today in social service and development circles, and I use it carefully. Development projects are expected to "empower" participants so that they can be independent agents of their own fates. People controlling their own project or development venture is a goal shared by both conservative and radical agents, though obviously with different motivations.

But what does it mean to empower or be empowered? At a very general level, it refers to people gaining the authority or the ability to choose more of what they want, are, do, and can be. It is possible to see empowerment also in terms of how people respond to, or are affected by, the chance occurrences and conditions of their lives. Empowerment can also be considered the means by which people as individuals or societies as a whole are enabled to function equitably. The notion of empowerment assumes that there are powerless people in society, mainly the poor, who feel and are treated as if they are objects being acted upon by their environment rather than subjects acting in and on their world.

However, the experience of empowering people exposes complexities and ambiguities. Sometimes it is not clear how a CED enterprise can help empower people. While it remains an important overall goal for any CED venture, empowerment is an amorphous and evolving standard for determining how successful an effort is in liberating people from psychological, cultural, economic, and political constraints or in creating the conditions necessary for their emancipation.

Others have written extensively about different kinds and levels of power. For example, Nelson and Wright describe three models of power to analyse participation and empowerment in development projects. The first model, called "power to" is described as a human growth model that assumes that people develop the "capacities and knowledge" to grow personally and collectively. At a personal level, this involves developing such liberating characteristics as confidence. This level of power also affects how people can "negotiate and influence close relationships" and work collectively "to have a greater impact than if one worked alone." The "power over" model involves gaining access to "political" decision making to expand abilities "to influence ever more aspects of their lives. . . . The challenge is for marginalized groups to gain treatment as equal partners in a process of development from people in such institutions, so that they have long-term access to resources and decision-making." A third model (which could be considered "power throughout") asserts that power is not a substance possessed and exercised by a person or an institution, but "is an apparatus consisting of discourse, institutions, actors and a flow of events" (Nelson and Wright 1995, 8).

For many years, community development projects sought to increase the "power to" and the "power over" aspects of projects for beneficiaries through various levels of participation in these development efforts. The essential thinking was that the more people participate, the more they get involved in these development efforts, and the more they could benefit and be empowered. This was an assumed aspect of the theory behind the formation of the Oodi Weavers and why the Canadian NGOs supported the project. The project was not meant to merely provide a job for these few workers. It was also intended to help the workers and other villagers gain control over their circumstances in sustained and self-directed ways.

Some development projects focused on "participation in implementation": people were actively encouraged and mobilized to take part in the actualization of projects. They were given certain responsibilities and set certain tasks or were required to contribute specified resources. Other projects focused on "participation in evaluation": at the completion of each phase of a project, people were invited to critique the success or failure of the initiative; in other words, they decided how useful the project was in meeting their needs or desires. Evaluation was a means of putting the results of a project in the hands of the people most important to that initiative. This type of participation would influence how such a project would be maintained and what beneficiaries could acquire for other activities in their lives.

A third type of participation was "participation in benefit": people would enjoy the fruits of a project, whether it was reticulated water, improved medical care, or a new community hall. The material results were considered the real measure of how people would be empowered, regardless of their involvement in planning or implementation.

A fourth participatory ideal, "participation in decision making," sought the most overt political path to empowerment. In these cases, people were expected to discuss, conceptualize, initiate, and plan activities they wanted and determined were necessary. In these efforts, empowerment was a central goal and procedural resource, as the authority and capacity to choose were cultivated and nurtured over time and through practice.

While one can argue that all of these approaches empower people in some way, we still do not know how effective these different formal strategies are. The actual process of empowering people is much more complex than the theoretical definitions imply, since there are no pure demarcations and directions. In case after case, we have found that efforts that were insensitive to people's needs, that were not participatory, still generated a motivation that led people to take control of a situation or process and empower themselves. In other cases we have seen dependencies perpetuated even when the projects were built from a genuine desire for independence and sound participatory planning.

Part of the difficulty in determining how empowerment occurs is in understanding the situational dynamics and elements that affect relations of power and how these relations change. Each situation is influenced by the problems and obstacles, or solutions and opportunities faced by participants; and things seen as assets in some situations could be considered restraints in others. For example, poor participants may need to see their economic situation improve before they participate in a more socially oriented, empowering enterprise. This in turn may lead to conflict with the more economically powerful elements in their communities, which can create new obstacles to empowerment.

The nature of outside intervention will also affect the process of empowerment. Often a participatory or empowering process will be initiated by a leadership whose vision may be foreign to the people concerned, but eventually accepted. Outsiders with honourable intentions may intervene and inadvertently disrupt situations, though objectively they may be able to help the disempowered people who are involved. As well, while there may be a need for external assistance, it must be balanced with the need for self-reliance to avoid creating new dependencies. Often, some form of organization is a prerequisite for empowerment because the forces keeping people poor or powerless are largely external to their local situation. Care must be exercised to ensure that these organizations do not become centres of formal power controlled by the few, with new controls placed on CED participants.

In short, initiatives to promote participation cannot be based on externally defined standards, goals, or strategies. Ultimately, it may only be possible to create the conditions for people to empower themselves. And each situation has to be approached incrementally, flexibly, and in such a way that the people most in need are able to influence or control what they do throughout an evolving process of learning and acting.

Weavers in Control

In general, the weavers are dealing with the dimensions of power in practical daily ways defined through the various theories of participation. They are taking seriously the ownership of their firm and are exercising some control. Some of the Cooperative members have even taken their participation in their factory to the levels of control that the project was designed to provide. These workers are exercising their power of choice, which could include not taking action in certain situations. They are deciding who they will or will not work with, and non-members cannot force decisions onto the Cooperative.

For now, I think it is evident that the workers are pressured by circumstances and organizational deficiencies into accepting a weak management. Therefore, they are making a choice. They will choose to change their management when the opportunities presented to them appear viable. As an outsider I believe this change is overdue, but it must and will be the workers who determine when this change is appropriate for them.

Ultimately they will either benefit or suffer from this exercise of control, but that is the way it should be for any CED venture. The weavers' authority over their enterprise must be coupled with responsibility for their actions, to ensure a greater possibility that they will act in their own best interests. Authority without responsibility merely creates a facade of empowerment that can crumble under pressure.

I believe this was an essential perspective that Ulla and Peder Gowenius inculcated into every aspect of the project. The way the workers determine their wages, share management duties, and make decisions about innovations such as a nursery were all developed so that the workers not only had authority over these issues, but also would concretely gain or lose by how the issues were handled. As Peder said, "If you are concerned about changing this country, developing it, then things like the management committee, decentralization of decision making and a broad educational programme are required. The way we do things in the factory is not only because of ideology, but because it is the only practical way, the only way of getting things done and the only way of really helping this country."

What is fundamentally taking place in these CED ventures is the transformation in the nature and exercise of power; a transformation in the way people assert their interests and desires in relation to themselves, each other, and the world around them. This transformation is an amorphous and convoluted process, often camouflaged by conventional cultural behaviour, tossed about by dominant relations of power that are obviously reluctant to change, and viewed through various perceptions based on conflicting interests.

This book has not delved extensively into the personal levels and manifestations of power that the workers — the women, in particular — have acquired. That would be another book. I have only touched on a few of the relations between the weavers and their village, and the contradictions between what the workers have been empowered to do in their Cooperative and what their cultural life has allowed them to do. While this is an important aspect of a CED enterprise, it also means deeply understanding the cultural dimensions of power and change.

The weavers have made significant strides within the confines of their Cooperative, learning about and exercising power over their work and how they interact with others. This power is not absolute and it has not always been exercised in their best interests. But they have a basic control of their workplace and their productivity, and they are responsible to and for themselves in ways that most workers in Botswana (and, I speculate, around the world) can only dream of. What they have acquired in terms of material assets, knowledge, and personal experience will benefit them in numerous and continuing ways.

To the credit of the Cooperative members, of the people who set up the project 25 years ago, and of all the others who helped the weavers over the years, the most important aspect of the project has been achieved — Oodi Weavers belongs to the workers.

Bibliography

Abell, Peter, and Nicholas Mahoney
   1988   *Small-Scale Industrial Cooperatives in Developing Countries*, Oxford:
          Oxford University Press.
Adams, Frank, and Gary Hansen
   1996   "Education for Ownership and Participation," in Krimerman and
          Lindenfeld (eds.), *When Workers Decide*, Philadelphia: New Society
          Publishers.
African Development Bank
   1993   "Annual Report 1993," London: Intermediate Technology Publications.
Aggleton, A., and T. Bertozzi
   1995   *Socio-Economic Impact of HIV/AIDS on Households*, Geneva: World
          Health Organization.
Bank of Botswana
   1996   "Annual Report 1995," Gaborone: Bank of Botswana.
Barnett, T., and P. Blaikie
   1992   *AIDS in Africa: Its Present and Future Impact*, London: Bell Haven.
Botswana Institute of Development Policy Analysis
   1997   "Study of Poverty and Poverty Alleviation in Botswana, Phase 1," Vol.
          1, Gaborone: BIDPA.
Brodhead, Dal
   1994   "CED Practice in Canada," in Galaway and Hudson.
Chotani, Harish
   1995   "Organization Analysis of Lentswe la Oodi Weavers," Gaborone:
          Women's Finance House Botswana.

Cooperation for Research, Development and Education
1989 "An Evaluation of SIDA Support to Lentswe la Oodi Producers Cooperative Society Limited," Gaborone: CORDE.

Curry, R. L.
1987 "Poverty and Mass Unemployment in Mineral Rich Botswana" in *American Journal of Economics and Sociology*, Vol. 46, No. 1.

CUSO
1987 "Botswana/Saskatchewan Tapestry Tour 1987," Regina: CUSO.

Douglas, David
1994 *Community Economic Development in Canada*, Vols. 1 and 2, Toronto: University of Toronto Press.

Dulansey, Maryanne, and James Austin
1985 "Small-scale Enterprise and Women," in Catherine Overholt, Mary Anderson, Kathleen Cloud and James Austin, eds., *Gender Roles in Development Projects*, Connecticut: Kumarian Press.

Duncan, T., K. Jefferis and P. Molutsi
1994 *Social Development in Botswana: A Retrospective Analysis*, Gaborone: Government of Botswana/UNICEF.

Fairbairn, Brett, et al. (eds)
1991 *Cooperatives and Community Development: Economics in Social Perspective*, Saskatoon: Centre for the Study of Cooperatives.

Farrington, D. J., Lewis S. Satish and A. Miclat-Teves (eds.)
1993 *Non-Governmental Organizations and the State in Asia*, London: Routledge.

Frank, Flo
1994 "Training — An Urgent Community Economic Development Need," in Galaway and Hudson.

Galaway, Burt, and Joe Hudson
1994 *Community Economic Development: Perspectives on Research and Policy*, Toronto: Thompson Educational Publishing.

Government of Botswana
1997 "Botswana Human Development Report, 1997," Gaborone: UNDP.

Government of Botswana
1997 *Community-Based Strategy for Rural Development*, Gaborone: Ministry of Finance and Development Planning.

Government of Botswana
1995 "Policy on Women in Development," Gaborone: Ministry of Labour and Home Affairs.

Government of Botswana, Central Statistics Office
1991 *A Poverty Datum Line for Botswana*, Gaborone: Ministry of Finance and Development Planning.

Government of Botswana, NDP7
1991 *Seventh National Development Plan (NDP7), 1991-97*, Gaborone: Ministry of Finance and Development Planning.

Government of Botswana/UNICEF/UNDP
1993 "Planning for People: A strategy for Accelerated Human Development in Botswana," Gaborone: Ministry of Finance and Development Planning.

Gowenius, Peder
    1972   Proposal for Establishing a Weaving Centre, submitted to Canadian
           Universities Service Overseas and Botswana Christian Council, October.
Grant, Elinah, and Sandy Grant
    1995   *Decorated Homes in Botswana*, Gaborone: Phuthadikobo Museum.
Harper, Malcolm
    1992   *Their Own Idea: Lessons from Workers Cooperatives*, London: Intermediate
           Technology Publications.
Harvey, C., and S. R. Lewis
    1990   *Policy Choice and Development Performance in Botswana*, New York: St-
           Martin Press.
Harvey, Charles
    1992   "Is the Economic Miracle Over?" Institute of Development Studies,
           Discussion Paper No. 298, Sussex, February.
Hedenquist, J. A.
    1992   *Introduction to Social and Community Development in Botswana*,
           Gaborone: Ministry of Local Government and Lands (Botswana),
           Government Printer.
Humphrey, John, and Hubert Schmilz
    1996   "Trust and Economic Development," Discussion Paper No. 355,
           Institute for Development Studies, Sussex, August.
International Monetary Fund
    1995   *International Financial Statistics*, Washington: IMF.
Jefferis, K.
    1993   "Botswana's Industrialization Policy and its Implications for Regional
           Economic Corporation." A paper presented to the Economic Research
           Unit and Department of Economics, University of Natal Durban, South
           Africa, May.
Kaufman, Michael, and Haroldo Dilla Alfonso
    1997   *Community Power and Grassroots Democracy: The Transformation of Social
           Life*, London: ZED Books.
Kaunda, M., and K. Miti
    1995   "Promotion of Private Enterprise and Citizen Entrepreneurship in
           Botswana," in *Development Southern Africa*, Vol. 12, No. 3, Gaborone.
Landell-Mills, P.
    1973   Letter from the Ministry of Finance and Development Planning to
           Peder Gowenius.
Lewis, Stephen, and Jennifer Sharpley
    1988   "Botswana's Industrialization," Discussion Paper No. 245, Institute for
           Development Studies, Sussex, June.
Lewycky, Dennis
    1981   *Tapestry, Report from Oodi Weavers*, Gaborone: University of Botswana,
           National Institute for Research in Development and African Studies,
           Documentation Unit, 1977 and.
Major, G. A.
    1973   Letter to the Permanent Secretary, Ministry of Finance and
           Development Planning.

McCarthy, Stephen
  1994 *Africa: The Challenge of Transformation*, London: I. B. Tauris.
Mills, Ann Newdigat
  1987 "Botswana/Saskatchewan Tapestry Tour 1987," Regina: Canadian Universities Service Overseas.
Moffat, Linda, Yolande Geadah and Rieky Stuart
  1991 *Two Halves Make a Whole: Balancing Gender Relations in Development*, Ottawa: Canadian Council for International Cooperation and MATCH International Centre.
Mogome-Ntsatsi, Kgomotso
  1989 *Needs and Participation in Rural Development: A Study of Extension Programmes in a Botswana Village*, Gaborone: University of Botswana Ph.D. Thesis.
Mwansa, L. K.
  1995 "Participation of Non-Governmental Organizations," in *Social Development Journal of Social Development in Africa*, Vol. 10, No. 1.
Mwansa, P. Chalwe
  1995 "Neighbours Wary of South Africa's Trade Protectionism," *Business Focus,* Vol.2, No. 3, October.
Nelson, Nici, and Susan Wright
  1995 *Power and Development, Theory and Practice*, London: Intermediate Technology Publications.
Nthomang, Keitseope, and Morena Rankopo
  1997 "Integrated Community Economic Development in Botswana," in Eric Shragge, *Community Economic Development.*
Picard, Louis A.
  1985 *The Politics of Development in Botswana: A Model for Success?* London: Lynne Rienner Publishers.
Schmitz, Hubert
  1989 "Flexible Specialization — a New Paradigm of Small Scale Industrialization," Discussion Paper No. 261, Institute for Development Studies, Sussex, May.
Shragge, Eric
  1997 *Community Economic Development: In Search of Empowerment (second edition)*, Montréal: Black Rose Books.
Stoneman, Colin, and Carol Thompson
  1992 "SADCC — The Realistic Hope for Southern Africa," *The Courier,* No. 134, July–August.
Waring, Marilyn
  1988 *If Women Counted: A New Feminist Economics*, NY: Harper.